Conversations with Jay Parini

Literary Conversations Series
Peggy Whitman Prenshaw
General Editor

Conversations
with Jay Parini

Edited by Michael Lackey

University Press of Mississippi   *Jackson*

www.upress.state.ms.us

The University Press of Mississippi is a member
of the Association of American University Presses.

Library of Congress Cataloging-in-Publication Data
Conversations with Jay Parini / edited by Michael Lackey.
    pages cm. — (Literary Conversations Series)
  Summary: "This book contains the most important interviews with Jay Parini, who is best
known for his 1990 The Last Station, a multi-perspective novel about Leo Tolstoy's last year.
But he has also published numerous volumes of poetry; biographies of William Faulkner,
Robert Frost, and John Steinbeck; novels; and literary and cultural criticism. Parini's work is
valuable not just because of its high quality and intellectual range. It is crucial for understanding late-20th and early-21st century literature more generally, as Parini not only engages in a
lively conversation with other prominent writers, but also was close friends with so many of
these authors. He has openly written poems in conversation with such writers as Robert Penn
Warren, Gore Vidal, Jorge Luis Borges, and others. He has had an ongoing conversation with
many literary friends over the years—Alastair Reid, Seamus Heaney, Anne Stevenson, Ann
Beattie, Julia Alvarez, Peter Ackroyd, A. N. Wilson, and countless others. His life often seems
like a seminar table, with friends gathered, talking, trading stories. These interviews will give
scholars a more comprehensive understanding of his work as a poet, scholar, public intellectual, literary critic, intellectual historian, biographer, novelist, and biographical novelist. More
importantly, these interviews will contribute to our understanding of the history of ideas, the
condition of knowledge, and the state of literature, which Parini has played an important role
in shaping"— Provided by publisher.
  Includes index.
  ISBN 978-1-62846-025-4 (hardback) — ISBN 978-1-62846-026-1 (ebook) 1. Parini, Jay—Interviews. 2. Authors, American—20th century—Interviews. I. Lackey, Michael.
  PS3566.A65Z46 2014
  813'.54—dc23
  [B]   2013044468

British Library Cataloging-in-Publication Data available

Books by Jay Parini

Singing in Time. Dundee (Scotland): J. W. B. Laing, 1972.
Theodore Roethke: An American Romantic. Amherst, MA: University of Massachusetts Press, 1979.
The Love Run. Boston: Little, Brown, 1980.
Anthracite Country. New York: Random House, 1982.
The Patch Boys. New York: Henry Holt, 1986.
Town Life. New York: Henry Holt, 1988.
The Last Station. New York: Henry Holt, 1990.
Bay of Arrows. New York: Henry Holt, 1992.
John Steinbeck: A Biography. New York: Henry Holt, 1995.
Benjamin's Crossing. New York: Henry Holt, 1996.
Some Necessary Angels: Essays on Literature and Politics. New York: Columbia University Press, 1997.
House of Days. New York: Henry Holt, 1998.
Robert Frost: A Life. New York: Henry Holt, 1999.
The Apprentice Lover. New York: HarperCollins, 2002.
Passage to Liberty: The Story of Italian Immigration and the Rebirth of America, with A. Kenneth Ciongoli. New York: Random House, 1992.
One Matchless Time: A Life of William Faulkner. New York: HarperCollins, 2004.
The Art of Teaching. New York: Oxford University Press, 2005.
The Art of Subtraction: New and Selected Poems. New York: Braziller, 2005.
Why Poetry Matters. New Haven, CT: Yale University Press, 2008.
Promised Land: Thirteen Books that Changed America. New York: Doubleday, 2008.
The Passages of H.M. New York: Doubleday, 2010. (London: Canongate).
Jesus: The Human Face of God. New York: Houghton Mifflin, 2013

Contents

Introduction

In the afterword to the biographical novel *The Last Station*, when discussing the method of research he used to write his multi-perspective narrative account of Leo Tolstoy's final year, Jay Parini explains how reading in succession numerous diaries from members of Tolstoy's inner circle "was like looking at a constant image through a kaleidoscope." It was this response that he hoped to replicate in his reader through the narrative form of *The Last Station*, for he "soon fell in love with the continually changing symmetrical forms of life that came into view" (289). But in addition to his research, Parini's friendship with Gore Vidal led him to construct his multi-perspective narrative approach to Tolstoy's life. During a conversation about historical fiction, Vidal urged Parini "to put Tolstoy at the still center of the novel and to revolve my characters around him as a cubist painting" ("Mentors" 16).

This brief description of the genesis of *The Last Station*'s narrative form tells an important story about Parini's centrality to late-twentieth and early-twenty-first century American and European letters. Parini has made a significant contribution to the development of the contemporary biographical novel in such works as *The Last Station* (1990), *Benjamin's Crossing* (1996), and *The Passages of H.M.* (2010). But to understand the nature of his contribution, it is important to see how he has simultaneously built on and distanced himself from some of America's literary luminaries—including Vidal and Robert Penn Warren, who were both friends. For instance, Warren published in 1946 *All the King's Men*, a novel modeled on the life of Huey Long that illuminates the historical situation and the political psychology in the South during the 1930s. To give himself more creative license, Warren changed Long's name to Willie Stark, a move common among historical novelists. To Parini, Warren was as much a mentor as a friend. But what is significant is the degree to which Parini locates his work within the same tradition as but also distances himself from Warren. As Parini claims in my interview with him:

In *All the King's Men*, written in the mid-forties, Robert Penn Warren felt tightly bound to the traditions of conventional historical fiction. I don't think he could see his way toward the contemporary forms of the biographical novel, or else he would have called his protagonist Huey Long, not Willie Stark. I wish he had. I think he could have written a better novel if he'd actually dug into Long, because I know he was obsessed with him. I had detailed conversations with him about Long.

For Parini, something in Warren's understanding of history prohibited him from taking the novel to its next logical stage, which is the biographical form of the novel.

What makes Parini's work such a goldmine for scholars and theorists is his willingness and ability to illuminate literary history from many vantage points. When Vidal recommended that Parini construct a cubist novel, he was assisting Parini the biographical novelist. But Parini narrates that story in his book of literary criticism, *Some Necessary Angels: Essays on Writing and Politics*. So it is Parini the literary critic who sheds significant light on the narrative form of a biographical novel such as *The Last Station*. That Vidal inspired Parini to use a cubist narrative form in *The Last Station*, an aesthetic choice that sets Parini's work apart from Vidal's biographical novels *Burr* and *Lincoln*, and that Parini sees *The Last Station* as advancing the form of the historical novel beyond the approach Warren deployed in *All the King's Men*, indicate the degree to which Parini is responding to as well as altering a well-established literary tradition.

While Parini's contributions to American letters are many and varied, as he is a first-rate poet, a well-respected critic, and a masterful novelist, I focus in this introduction on his work on the biographical novel because Parini has been a pioneer, as both a practitioner and theoretician, of this genre, which has become so immensely popular since the 1980s. Given Georg Lukacs's unambiguous condemnation of the biographical form of the novel in his landmark study *The Historical Novel* in the late 1930s, it would seem that few would be willing to write such works. But by the mid-eighties, there was a veritable explosion of biographical novels, such as Ron Hansen's *The Assassination of Jesse James by the Coward Robert Ford* (1983), Vidal's *Lincoln* (1984), Bruce Duffy's *The World As I Found It* (1987), Joanna Scott's *Arrogance* (1990), Irvin D. Yalom's *When Nietzsche Wept* (1992), Julia Alvarez's *In the Time of the Butterflies* (1994), Madison Smartt Bell's *All Souls' Rising* (1995), David Mamet's *The Old Religion* (1997), Anita Diamant's *The Red Tent* (1997), Michael Cunningham's *The Hours* (1998), Russell Banks's *Cloudsplit-*

ter (1998), Hansen's *Hitler's Niece* (1999), Joyce Carol Oates's *Blonde* (2000) Yalom's *The Schopenhauer Cure* (2005), Lance Olsen's *Nietzsche's Kisses* (2006), Edmund White's *Hotel de Dream* (2007), Sherry Jones's *The Jewel of Medina* (2008), M. Allen Cunningham's *Lost Son* (2008), Olsen's *Head in Flames* (2009), Duffy's *Disaster Was My God* (2011), Yalom's *The Spinoza Problem* (2012), and Rebecca Kanner's *The Sinners and the Sea* (2013). How can we account for this surge? What intellectual forces led these writers to dismiss or ignore Lukacs's prohibition regarding the biographical novel? And what is the aesthetic theory underwriting these novels? It is my contention that we will find more answers to these questions in the pages of Parini's biographical novels, literary criticism, and interviews than anywhere else.

The History of Ideas and the Idea of History

As an author of factual biographies (John Steinbeck, William Faulkner, and Robert Frost) and biographical novels, Parini is in a privileged position to clarify the difference between the two. He can explain precisely why one is more true than the other. Paradoxically, he suggests that there is more truth in fictional work than in factual biography. We get some insight into his thinking through his interview with Ramona Koval. As Parini says, "I'm interested in lives and I'm interested in fiction. I'm very close friends with the English writer Peter Ackroyd, we've been friends for years, and I once said to Peter, 'Peter, you've written a dozen novels and you've written a dozen biographies (Dickens, T. S. Eliot, William Blake). What's the difference, would you say, between your novels and your biographies?' And Peter said to me, 'Oh well, you see, in the novels I have to really tell the truth but in the biographies I just make it up.'" The traditional view is that there is a certain level of nonfictional transparency in the biography, which consists of unadulterated facts. Within this framework, fiction connotes falsity, that which is the opposite of fact (is it fact or fiction?). But something happened to disrupt this simple binary, and for Parini, that something is postmodernism.

Let me briefly contrast the work of Virginia Woolf and Parini in order to identify what happened in order for the biographical novel to be considered a legitimate possibility. As Woolf argues in her essay "The Art of Biography," the "novelist is free" to create, while "the biographer is tied" (120) to facts. Lytton Strachey and the new biographers of the early twentieth century revolutionized the biography by making liberal use of the creative imagination and fictional techniques in depicting a person's life, thus giving the artist/biographer the "freedom to invent" something new, "a book that was not only a biography but also a work of art" (123). But, ultimately, Woolf concluded, this "combination proved unworkable," because "fact and fiction refused to mix" (123).

For Parini, developments in postmodern theory made it possible to fuse biography and the novel. The opening sentences of his essay, "Fact or Fiction: Writing Biographies Versus Writing Novels," clarify one of the key ideas at the core of Parini's project: "The relationship between fact and fiction is vexed," thus calling into question "the nature of truth itself." Postmodern theory accounts for this development, which Parini defines: "although truth may be in some sense objective, most attempts to reconstruct or reflect that objectivity, whether in fiction or nonfiction, history or biography, are tainted by both the medium itself—language, and ideology, that matrix of assumptions and preconceptions that underlies every gesture in the direction of signification" (241). Since all discursive representations require a selection or organization of specific facts, a deletion or accentuation of certain details, and a synthesis or compartmentalization of external entities, all writing is, by definition, an act of fictionalization. Parini frequently underscores this point by noting that the word fiction "has its origins in the Latin *fictio*, which means 'shaping'" (244). Thus, Parini can only conclude: "The areas of fiction and nonfiction overlap in suggestive ways, creating a kind of wild zone in which disbelief is suspended and the narrative itself becomes all consuming" (244). To think that any person or discipline could stand outside of fiction is perhaps one of the most irresponsible fictions humans have ever concocted.

This postmodernist view impacted not only biography but also history. As Parini says in the round-table conversation "The Uses of History in the Biographical Novel," "History is fiction." Indeed, Parini goes so far as to challenge the historian's legitimacy: "I'm just wondering how any historians can justify their job. I mean, has somebody written the equivalent article, 'The Death of the Historian'? How is it actually possible to write history in this age? I don't know how. I don't know what any historian imagines he or she is doing except creating a work of fiction. It may be based on facts, but the historians are arranging and rearranging and shuffling and building narratives and looking for patterns." If it can be shown that historians use the same rhetorical strategies, devices, and techniques as creative writers in constructing their narratives, then it would no longer make sense to treat historical representations as any more truthful than narratives of fiction.

At this point, it seems that Parini is in a contradiction. If biography and history are fictions, then they would be able to express some of the deepest truths about their subject matter, because Parini argues that fiction is more truthful than biography and/or history. But here we need to distinguish how the word fiction functions in different contexts in Parini's writings. All writing, whether historical, philosophical, biographical, scientific, or psychological, is fiction, because converting external phenomena into sign systems necessitates a selective arrangement of semiotic facts and conceptual relations. So when Parini says that biography and history are mere fictions, he is trying to expose their more-than-fiction pretensions as uninformed nonsense. Fiction, in this context, is meant to degrade, to take history and biography out of the fantasy realm of the Ideal Form and bring them down to earth. By stark contrast, when Parini uses fiction to refer to established forms of literature, such as poetry and the novel, the word has a positive connotation. For Parini, "if you really want to find out what happens . . . What happened in our history . . . You really go to a fiction writer." The question, of course, is this: what can the fiction writer give readers that the historian and/or the biographer cannot?

Biographers and historians focus on empirical facts, and while fiction writers certainly reference and respect such facts, they focus more on human interiors, the world of motivations and the unconscious. As Parini says in his interview with Paul Holler: "Fiction allows you more freedom: you can imagine motives, dig into the unconscious of a character, go inside a character's head." It would seem that Parini, who knows the work of Jacques Derrida, Roland Barthes, and J. Hillis Miller, would have some reservations about claiming to know the interior worlds of people such as Herman Melville, Leo Tolstoy, and Walter Benjamin, the subjects of his three biographical novels. But those who think that the lesson of postmodernism was to stop imagining the interior worlds of historical figures have drawn the wrong conclusion.

After denying the existence of metaphysical truth, postmodernists have gone in two separate directions. Deconstructionists, having embraced the radical indeterminacy of meaning, foreground gaps in knowledge, fragments of meaning, and the incoherence of metanarratives. Therefore, they see all texts as doing essentially the same thing: perpetually deferring meaning by underscoring how texts ultimately showcase their own deconstructive contradictions. Ironically, most deconstructionists derived many of their views from Nietzsche but failed to grasp the logical implications of his work. (Paul de Man's *Allegories of Reading* is the perfect case in point.) Nietzsche, like the poststructuralists, deconstructs the traditional correspondence theory of truth. The world is no longer a readable text that humans are tasked with deciphering. Nietzsche notes that modern historiographers understood the implications of the deconstruction of the correspondence theory of truth, which is why they concluded that it is impossible to 'prove' anything about the nature of history or the world. But from this insight, "modern historiography" drew the wrong (nihilistic) conclusion, for "it no longer wishes to 'prove' anything; it disdains to play the judge and considers this a sign of good taste—it affirms as little as it denies; it ascertains, it 'describes' . . . All this is to a high degree ascetic; but at the same time it is to an even higher degree *nihilistic*" (*Genealogy* 157). Parini would certainly agree with Nietzsche, for while he also rejects the *liber-mundi* approach to the world, he considers it a mistake to stop formulating systems of truth about life, the human, and the world. It is for this reason that Parini considers deconstruction "a blind alley of sorts, because the deconstructed text often dissolved into an endless series of 'traces'—fragments of meaning like meteors streaking through the night sky and disappearing" ("Lessons" 208). Parini is certainly sympathetic to Derrida's deconstruction of metaphysical truth and his destabilization of binary opposites, but he is simply unwilling to join the many desconctructionists who believe that this is the final word about truth and meaning.

For Parini, Richard Rorty, the American pragmatist philosopher, offers a more useful, positive, and meaningful response to the death of metaphysical truth. In a lecture that he delivered at the University of Minnesota, Morris, Parini explains how Rorty's approach to truth enabled him to clarify his objectives as a novelist. For Rorty, truth does not objectively mirror objective reality, because there is no such thing as objective reality. Therefore, literature cannot hope to reflect the world accurately. Rather, the "novelist creates the context for truth, embodies social truth." In a conversation, Rorty told Parini "what novelists and poets were trying to 'do' with truth." Rorty said: "'Just think of language as picks and shovels. You decide where to dig. You dig. What you find will be yours to recognize, and you'll recognize what you find and give it truth, in your own way.'" Truth may not be absolute or metaphysical, but that does not mean that humans should stop constructing truth systems. As beings with "an instinctive need . . . to keep meaning within controlled boundaries" ("Lessons" 206), Parini insists on creating truth in and through literature. But it must be a truth that calls attention to itself as fiction, that vigorously resists the impulse to pawn itself off as metaphysical or absolute.

Given his contention that all truth is fiction, Parini turns the conventional wisdom about the biographical novel and historical fiction on its head.

Many novels are about human lives, but because they alter certain facts or fail to represent the whole of people's lives, authors frequently preface their works with the following proviso: "'The characters in this novel are entirely fictitious and any relation to persons living or dead is certainly accidental.'" Parini urges future novelists to stop making this claim and instead to say: "'Everything in the following pages is authentic, which is to say it is as true as I could make it. Take it or leave it'" ("Fact" 250). Since all writing is now understood to be fiction, there is no need to preface biographical novels or historical fiction with traditional disclaimers. The task, rather, is to identify and define the kind of truth that each genre of writing seeks to represent.

For Parini, what makes the contemporary biographical novel superior to other works is the truth it depicts, which is the subconscious structure of meaning that underwrites a character, a culture, and their politics. This is a view that he got from Vidal. As Parini says in his "Mentors" essay, Vidal "often alludes to Alfred North Whitehead, who said that one got to the essence of a culture not by looking at what is said but by looking at what is not said, the underlying assumptions of the society, too obvious to be stated. Truth—or some crucial aspect of truth—resides in those silences" (15–16). The task of the novelist is to inhabit and represent a character's or a society's subconscious in order to identify, define, and chart the unacknowledged logics and ideologies that predetermine historical events, discursive systems, and patterns of relations. And when novelists succeed in doing this, they give their readers more substantial truth about people, culture, and history than any other intellectual professional.

A Novel Theory of Redemption

Central to Parini's aesthetic is imagining "a politics of redemption" ("Imagination" 230). Within this framework, the novelist must do two separate things: expose the subconscious structures that make oppression possible and imagine alternative structures. The objective is not simply to picture a particular consciousness. It is also to "shift consciousness in significant ways" (227). This, in part, explains why Parini had to reject the classical historical novel and to embrace the postmodern biographical novel. For instance, in his biographical novel *Benjamin's Crossing*, Parini suggests that, to understand major historical collisions, knowledge of a culture's dominant structures of consciousness is imperative. It is important to note, however, that structures of consciousness are provisional. In *Benjamin's Crossing* there are two separate structures, one that made the Holocaust possible, and one that would have rendered the Nazis' anti-Semitic ideology incoherent, thus disabling it.

The subconscious structure of consciousness that dominated Nazi Germany is one premised on a metaphysics of identity, which holds that there is an ontological distinction between Germans and Jews. For Parini, this approach to identity is not a metaphysical fact of racial or ethnic being. Rather, it is an epistemological presupposition, which is both incoherent and needs to be deconstructed. Ironically, it was not only the Nazis who subscribed to this view. Prominent Jews, such as Gershom Scholem, who was Benjamin's close friend, also adopted it. Throughout the novel, Scholem pressures his friend to get a clear "sense of his own Jewishness" (5). But Benjamin rejects the idea of a definable Jewish identity, not because he is a self-loathing Jew, but because he is a postmodernist, who has totally discarded the idea of a metaphysics of identity. In a moment of reflection, he concludes: "My selves are many, he thought. One by one they emerge in my letters. They are all true, even when contradictory. I embrace them all" (130). There is no single identity that subsumes all others. To the contrary, the self is composed of many identities, some that are even in conflict with each other.

What made the Nazi system possible was an implicit and naïve belief in metaphysics, the view that there are truths (a metaphysical definition of the German, a metaphysical definition of a Jew, and a metaphysical constellation relating the two) that are valid for all people in all places at all times. Having understood not just the absurdities but also the dangers of metaphysics, it only makes sense that Parini's Benjamin adamantly rejects it. And he does this after having a conversation with Bertolt Brecht, in which Brecht makes the case for a nontechnical form of simplified thinking. Reflecting on Brecht's claim, Benjamin says to himself: "The elaborate metaphysical turns that had become second nature to him through long years of philosophical study must be sacrificed now" (131). Benjamin rejects Scholem's approach to identity, primarily because Scholem unwittingly adopted the same metaphysical structure of consciousness as Hitler and the Nazis.

If metaphysics is the subconscious structure that enabled the Nazis to define Jews as the other and to justify their atrocities against them, then it is a concept of crossing that would effectively deconstruct metaphysics and thereby offer an alternative possibility for political redemption. As an anti-metaphysical thinker, Benjamin subscribes to a crossing approach to concepts and identities, which is why the title of Parini's book is so important. We get the best definition of crossing through a reference to a character named Meir Winklemann, who desired to become a rabbi, but because of a bad marriage, became a salesman. Given his career, Winklemann is described as "crossing borders so blithely that he no longer believed in the existence of separate countries" (72). With a clear understanding of European history and conceptual crossing, the idea of pure and fixed identities is totally absurd. Fluid, intermingling, blending—these are the things of which human and conceptual identity are composed, and necessarily so. For Scholem and the Nazis, to think that they could disentangle and/or differentiate German from Jew is more an adolescent fantasy than an incoherent fiction, for such distinctions are premised on the neat and tidy thinking (metaphysics) of a bygone era. And were Scholem or the Nazis to understand the implications of living in a post-metaphysical age, in the age of conceptual crossing, the whole metaphysical project underwriting the Nazi agenda would be exposed as nonsense.

There are many reasons why *Benjamin's Crossing* is such an important work, but what I want to emphasize here is its significance within the context of literary history. Put simply, Parini's work effectively counters Lukacs's work on the historical novel and offers an alternative. As an heir of Enlightenment rationalism, Lukacs favors a form of historical positivism that uses deterministic models to foreground a logical and rational causal nexus in history. Lukacs seeks "a clear understanding of history as a process, of history as the concrete precondition of the present" (21). Consequently, here is the right way to do the historical novel: "A writer who deals with history cannot chop and change with his material as he likes. Events and destinies have their natural, objective weight, their natural, objective proportion. If a writer succeeds in producing a story which correctly reproduces these relationships and proportions, then human and artistic truth will emerge alongside the historical. If, on the other hand, his story distorts these proportions, then it will distort the artistic picture as well" (290). In the forum titled "The Uses of History in the Biographical Novel," which is included in this volume, Parini explicitly rejects Lukacs's model, and it was his work on Benjamin that helped him to clarify why. For Parini, Lukacs adopted a "totalizing historical" perspective, which was reliant upon a form of "historical positivism" that could accurately picture objective reality. Benjamin, by contrast, "was an early thinker who was of many minds at once and who understood that there is no such thing as objective reality. There is only, as he said, the layering of subjective realities. My own work as a novelist has always involved the layering of subjective realities, trying to enter into these different subjectivities." In the pages of *Benjamin's Crossing*, Parini implicitly makes the case for a post-metaphysical model of conceptual crossing, which would effectively disable the metaphysics of meaning underwriting Nazi ideology and create the conditions for a more realistic and humane politics, that is, a politics of redemption.

Conversational Poetics

Given the dominance of Harold Bloom's anxiety-of-influence model of poetics, which came to prominence during Parini's most formative years as a writer, it would seem that he would have a need to ruin the sacred truths of his literary forebears, to engage in a form of literary warfare to the metaphorical death in order to assert his own will to poetic power. But early in his reading life, as a graduate student in Scotland, Parini developed a relationship to literature that is very different from the one found in Bloom's agonistic poetics. Obsessed by "Tradition and the Individual Talent," an early essay in which T. S. Eliot talks about how new work should operate in subtle conversation with the past, Parini always argues in his essays that literature is a form of conversation, and that a writer should modify and extend that tradition. In some ways, his biographical novels engage Tolstoy, Benjamin, and Melville in a kind of free-flowing conversation. That is not quite the case in the biographies of Steinbeck or Frost or Faulkner, where the conventions of the genre limit the possibilities, although even there one sees that Parini yearns to open a conversation, to engage in a kind of creative dialogue with one of his predecessors. He has openly written poems in conversation with writers he knew personally: Warren, Vidal, Jorge Luis Borges, and others. He has, in his own life, had an ongoing conversation with many literary friends over the years—Alastair Reid, Seamus Heaney, Anne Stevenson, Ann Beattie, Julia Alvarez, Peter Ackroyd, A. N. Wilson, and countless others. His life often seems like a seminar table, with friends gathered, talking, trading stories. His work offers a response to these conversations, even a continuation of them.

We get a clear sense of Parini's poetics in his poem, "A Conversation in Oxford," which was written in memory of his friend Isaiah Berlin, a prominent twentieth-century historian of ideas. The poem—which recalls one of many conversations that Parini had with Berlin when he was a fellow at Christ Church, Oxford, in the early nineties—centers on the "'weak foundations / of all human knowledge,'" which make a person "'shudder / to assume too much, to claim too boldly'" (8–10). In this poem, certain and dogmatic knowledge is a problem, not so much because it is no longer believable, but because it damages a person: it "can dull a heart, / occlude a mind, can chain a soul" (24-25). In the postmodern age, the "Big Ideas" have been exposed. They are not overarching ahistorical Truths that illuminate life and the world. They are "mostly preludes to deceit, / embodiments of someone's will-to-power" (28–30). Therefore, Berlin urges the narrator to find freedom "in gradations / dartings of the mind" (27–28). Within this framework, knowledge does not put the seeking soul at ease. To the contrary, it turns "us / loose upon ourselves" (36–37), leading us to an endless cycle of constructing and deconstructing our truths, our systems, our selves, for as the narrator says: "'We find ourselves / alive without a reason, inarticulate / but always trying to re-form a thought / in words that never seem quite right'" (46–49). We will never get to the final thought, the thought that no longer needs to be re-formed, for Berlin, who follows James Joyce's Stephen Dedalus, suggests that our world is now "ineluctably constructed upon the incertitude of the void" (572): "'The world is what you claim it is, / as well: this dwindling light, the smoke / of reason, ghostly words in ghostly air" (52–55). In an earlier age, this lack of an epistemological foundation would have been an occasion for despair, as we see in T. S. Eliot's *The Waste Land*, Ernest Hemingway's "A Clean, Well-Lighted Place," or Samuel Beckett's *Endgame*. If there is no ultimate Truth to make systematic sense of life, the human, and the world, then we are nothing more than nihilistic blips waiting for extinction. While Parini accepts the postmodern view that there is neither a metanarrative nor an ahistorical truth, he does not believe that this leads to nihilistic despair. In Parini's world, conversational words matter, even if they never rise to the level of an absolute truth, for they make us what we are, and they are a promise of what we can become:

> So I claim this hour, a plum-deep dusk,
> the need to pose so many questions,
> late, so late—an Oxford afternoon
> when everything but language falls away
> and words seem all the world we need. (56–60)

In the postmodern age, the conversations that enable us to set into motion the process of making and remaking ourselves in and through words is all we have. And yet, these are the very things worth claiming.

"A Conversation in Oxford" represents and enacts a shift in our understanding of the nature of knowledge, which leads to a significant transformation in the way artists respond to each other's work. To clarify the nature of this shift, let me briefly bring together the work of Parini and Rorty.

According to Rorty, traditional and analytic philosophers treat the concept like an immutable idea, an ahistorical precept "which philosophical analysis can hope to pin down." Rorty rejects this view, claiming that the concept is like a person, "never quite the same twice, always developing, always maturing" (21). Since Rorty rejects the existence of "an overarching ahistorical framework" (27), he sees philosophy, not in terms of a battle between philosophers to represent metaphysical reality, but in terms of a conversation that philosophers can and do have with one another (28). Such is Rorty's case for what he refers to as "conversational philosophy." According to this model, the task is not to prove that the precursor is wrong and that you are right. Rather, it is to engage in a respectful conversation in order to build a productive vision of human living. What Rorty encouraged philosophers to do in the early twenty-first century, Parini was already doing in his 1998 poem "A Conversation in Oxford." Parini does not need to degrade Berlin in order to establish his own system. Instead, he engages Berlin in a respectful conversation as he builds towards his own poetic vision. Put simply, the postmodern transformation of knowledge radically impacts the content and form of the aesthetic object and the way writers interact with their precursors, and it is in Parini's conversational poetics that we can best see the fruits of this model.

Parini's interviews will certainly give scholars a more comprehensive understanding of his work as a poet, scholar, public intellectual, literary critic, intellectual historian, biographer, novelist, and biographical novelist. But more importantly, these interviews will contribute to our understanding of the history of ideas, the condition of knowledge, and the state of literature, which Parini has played an important role in shaping.

Acknowledgments

I want to thank the University of Minnesota, Morris, and the University of Minnesota's Institute for Advanced Study for their support for this project. Without the University's generous financial assistance in securing two of the interviews, this book would not have been possible. I also want to thank the University of Minnesota, Morris, for providing me with my research assistants, Rachel Balzar and Kelsey Butler, who far exceeded my extremely high expectations. Finally, I would like to thank Jay, who has been very generous with his time and who continues to inspire.

ML

Works Cited

Benjamin, Walter. "Theses on the Philosophy of History," in *Illuminations*. Trans. Harry Zohn. New York: Schocken Books, 1968, 253–64.

Lukacs, Georg. *The Historical Novel*. Trans. Hannah and Stanley Mitchell. Lincoln and London: University of Nebraska Press, 1983.

Parini, Jay. *Benjamin's Crossing: A Novel*. New York: Henry Holt and Company, 1997.

———. "A Conversation in Oxford," in *The Art of Subtraction: New and Selected Poems*. New York: George Braziller, 2005.

———. "Fact or Fiction: Writing Biographies Versus Writing Novels," in *Some Necessary Angels*, 241–56.

———. "The Imagination of Politics," in *Some Necessary Angels*, 215–30.

———. "The Imagination of Truth: How Fiction Shines a Light into the Dark Corners of History," Barber Lecture at the University of Minnesota, Morris, September 19, 2012.

———. *The Last Station: A Novel of Tolstoy's Final Year*. New York: Anchor Books, 2009.

———. "The Lessons of Theory," in *Some Necessary Angels*, 203–14.

———. "Mentors," in *Some Necessary Angels*, 3–18.

———. *Some Necessary Angels: Essays on Writing and Politics*. New York: Columbia University Press, 1997.

Rorty, Richard. "Analytic and Conversational Philosophy," in *A House Divided: Comparing Analytic and Continental Philosophy*. Amherst, NY: Humanity Books, 2003.

Woolf, Virginia. "The Art of Biography," in *The Death of the Moth and Other Essays*. London: The Hogarth Press, 1942, 119–26.

Chronology

1948 Jay Parini is born in Pittston, Pennsylvania to Leo and Verna Parini.

1950 Parini's sister, Dorrie, is born.

1970 Graduates with an A.B. in History and Literature from Lafayette College.

1972 Publishes his first volume of poems *Singing in Time*.

1973 Completes the B.Phil. at the University of St. Andrews in Scotland.

1975 Receives his Ph.D. from the University of St. Andrews. Dartmouth College hires him as an assistant professor.

1976 Co-founds with Sydney Lea the *New England Review*.

1979 Publishes *Theodore Roethke: An American Romantic*.

1980 Publishes his novel *The Love Run*.

1981 Marries Devon Jersild.

1982 Publishes his poems *Anthracite Country*. Becomes D.E. Axinn Professor of English and Creative Writing at Middlebury College. His son, Will, is born.

1985 His son, Oliver, is born.

1986 Publishes his novel *The Patch Boys*.

1987 Publishes his textbook *An Invitation to Poetry*.

1988 Publishes his poems *Town Life*.

1990 Publishes his novel *The Last Station*.

1992 Publishes his novel *Bay of Arrows*.

1993 Receives a Guggenheim Fellowship. During the 1993-4 academic year, he is a Fowler Hamilton Fellow at Christ Church College, Oxford University.

1994 Edits the *Columbia History of American Poetry*. His son, Leo, is born.

1995 Edits the *Columbia Anthology of American Poetry*. Publishes *John Steinbeck: A Biography* and "The Greening of the Humanities" in *The New York Times Magazine*.

1996 Edits *Gore Vidal: Writer Against the Grain*. Publishes his novel *Benjamin's Crossing*.

1997 Publishes *Some Necessary Angels: Essays on Literature and Politics*.

Edits *Beyond "The Godfather": Italian American Writers on the Real Italian American Experience.*

1998   Publishes his poems *House of Days*. Edits *The Norton Book of American Autobiography.*

1999   Publishes *Robert Frost: A Life*. It wins the *Chicago Tribune*-Heartland Award for the year's best work on non-fiction.

2002   Publishes his novel *The Apprentice Lover*. Co-publishes with A. Kenneth Ciongoli *Passage to Liberty: The Story of Italian Immigration and the Rebirth of America.*

2004   Edits *The Oxford Encyclopedia of American Literature* and *World Writers in English*. Publishes *One Matchless Time: A Life of William Faulkner.*

2005   Publishes *The Art of Teaching* and *The Art of Subtraction: New and Selected Poems*. Edits *The Wadsworth Anthology of Poetry*. During the 2005-6 academic year, he is a fellow at the University of London's Institute for Advanced Studies.

2008   Publishes *Why Poetry Matters* and *Promised Land: Thirteen Books that Changed America.*

2009   Edits *Late Writings of Leo Tolstoy*. Michael Hoffman's film adaptation of Parini's novel *The Last Station* premiers with Christopher Plummer as Tolstoy and Helen Mirren as his wife Sofya. The film received two Academy-Award nominations, and the novel is translated into more than twenty-five languages.

2010   Publishes his novel *The Passages of H.M.*

2013   Publishes his biography *Jesus: The Human Face of God.*

Conversations with Jay Parini

The Poets—Strangers
on the Edge of Town

Tony Cannella / 1977

From the [Scranton] *Times-Tribune* (October 2, 1977). Reprinted by permission.

In the days of old, poets occupied center stage in their societies. Their epics and romances enthralled disparate audiences in village squares and royal courts. The lyrics they spun were not only passwords in their lovers' hearts but also their credentials for success—or at least success—in the workaday world. If a poet praised a king with panegyric, he was patronized and fed well. If he chose to lampoon the throne, he had the power to topple it or the privilege of losing his head in a noble cause. One way or another, the poet was heard. He counted.

And now, in the pragmatic ambience of technocratic society, where does the poet fit in?

For the most part, he doesn't. For poetry as an expression of mass appeal, the times are threadbare, with one possible exception—the emergence of women as a substantial part of the poet population.

In the words of Jay Parini, a twenty-nine-year-old poet who will soon return to his native Scranton for a reading of his works, "the contemporary poet often feels like a stranger at the edge of town. He wanders by himself, looking in, listening. His words ring in his or her own ears, and they may or may not find an audience. Poetry was once a language of communication, to some degree. Now it's really language in search of its deepest voice, an effort to discern its truest lineaments. Robert Frost called it 'the sound of sense.'"

Parini spoke from his office at Dartmouth College, in New Hampshire, where he is an assistant professor of English and director of the program in creative writing. "People look on poets as marginal figures. Once, centuries ago, poets occupied the center of culture. Poetry was the original form of literary expression, and our earlier major texts inhabit that form. I'm thinking of the *Iliad* and *Odyssey*. *Gilgamesh*, the great Sumerian epic. Or the Sanskrit epics, such as the *Ramayana*. Or the Hebrews *Psalms*—which is really the Norton Anthology of Hebrew lyrics, written by many hands. Nowadays, books of poetry are set aside, they rarely sell. But this might be a good thing, too. The lack of attention to poetry allows for a certain detachment. This is necessary for a poet's work. When W. H. Auden said that 'poetry makes nothing happen,' he put his finger on a good thing. Poetry lives far from the commercial world, and this unburdens it, to some extent. It makes its own way."

He talked about the landscape of his poetry. "Every poet has a private landscape at the back of his or her mind." For him, it's the Scranton region, Lackawanna County. He says, "It's not a faceless, monolithic suburb. It has a distinct culture, a richness—the old buildings, the terrain, the people. I often make use of the imagery of this region, find metaphors in the coal mines, the abandoned breakers, the culm dumps."

Parini's portraits of Scranton and Lackawanna County are not literal representations. They are distilled by imagination and the passage of time and they are representations of his youthful experiences here. As in "Walking the Trestle," which follows, a recollection of a time when he walked out alone on a train trestle, having taken a bet that he would do it, his friends taunting him as he walks out:

> They are all behind you, grinning
> with their eyes like dollars, their shouts
> of dare you, dare you, dare you
> broken by the wind. You squint ahead
> where the rusty trestle wavers into sky
> like a pirate's plank. And sun shines
> darkly on the Susquehanna, forty feet
> below. You stretch your arms
> to the sides of space and walk
> like a groom down that bare aisle.
> Out in the middle, you turn to wave
> and see their faces breaking like bubbles,
> the waves beneath you flashing coins,
> and all around you, chittering cables,
> birds, and the bright air clapping.

Parini says that "people are afraid of poetry these days, and with reason. A lot of it is simply bad or, less simply, complicated. Of course sometimes it has to be complicated. That's because life is complicated. But I like to imagine that poets can express this complication without confusing readers. Anyone who reads poetry will see that modern verse has become obsessively obscure, often without counterbalancing virtues. The virtues of good poetry aren't so different from those of a good person. I expect from myself and others clear, intelligent thinking, an honest approach to experience, and fresh language." Parini says that the definition of poetry he subscribes to was formulated by Gerard Manley Hopkins, the Jesuit poet. He called poetry "the common language heightened." "My poetry," says Parini, "is realistic more than anything else. It's easy to read, straightforward." Approximately half of his output has been in free verse, he says.

Some of the poets he admires are Robert Frost, Wallace Stevens, and Theodore Roethke. Like other writers, his work got published only after he "had tried a lot of times without success. I was rejected for years." He recalls: "I was helped by older writers in Scotland. I got my first acceptances in British magazines."

He says of northeastern Pennsylvania: "When I was living there, it was a bit depressing; but when I left the city and returned, after some years, I looked at it with new eyes. I had some critical detachment and a good deal of affection for the place."

Jay Parini Interview with Don Swaim

Don Swaim / 1990

From the Donald L. Swaim Collection, Mahn Center for Archives and Special Collections, Ohio University Libraries. Available from *Wired for Books*, WOUB Center for Public Media http://www.wiredforbooks.org/jayparini/ (August 16, 1990). Reprinted by permission.

Swaim: I really enjoyed your new book, *The Last Station*. It was terrific.
Parini: Thank you.

Swaim: You're teaching at Middlebury?
Parini: Middlebury College, yes. In Vermont. I've been there since 1982. Part of the furniture by now. They used to dust around me. Now they dust me as well.

Swaim: Well, let's talk about *The Last Station*. But first of all, I'd like to ask a couple of questions about you. You obviously know your Tolstoy. How did you become interested in this?
Parini: I've been reading Tolstoy since I was a teenager in high school, when I read *The Death of Ivan Ilyich*. It knocked me over, such a vivid piece of writing. This project—writing about Tolstoy—lay somewhere in the back of my mind for years, a smoldering interest that was only fanned into flames about five years ago, when I came across the diary of Valentin Bulgakov, Tolstoy's young secretary, in a bookstore in Italy—one of those chance things that produce large effects in your life. I grew more excited as I read, realizing that the last year of Tolstoy's life was an unusually dramatic and revelatory situation. This great figure in world literature had a lot going on in this last year or so, and this year was a kind of lens through which the tumultuous and moving events of his life filtered. I read that ten or more people were also keeping diaries during the last year of Tolstoy's life, and having read this one diary by Bulgakov, I wrote to someone at the Tolstoy Society in London asking if other diaries were available. I quickly managed to get many

of these, and I read through them in succession. A striking vision of reality emerged, as if seen through various pieces of a prism, producing a kaleidoscopic effect. I watched as this year unfolded from different aspects. I had found a novel here. All I had to do was to play with what emerged, orchestrating these voices into a kind of fugue. For compression, and artistic effect, I simplified the story by limiting it to six voices, one of them being Tolstoy's voice—always in his own words, another one being my voice, but mainly the other voices. I retold parts of the same story from shifting points of view.

Swaim: It's got everything a novel should have: love, sex, death, violence . . .
Parini: Tolstoy's life was full of these things. The contradictions seemed mind-boggling. By the end of his life, as you know, he'd become kind of a prophet. He had long ago given up fiction as a major piece of his writing life. He turned to religious, political, and ethical essays—on subjects such as world peace or vegetarianism. He became a guru of sorts, and identified with the poor, the oppressed. And there were a lot of these in Russia at this time. He believed one should be chaste and, in later years, rejected sexual relations within the context of a marriage: a theme in *The Kreutzer Sonata*. But he was a lusty guy.

Swaim: He had thirteen children.
Parini: A baker's dozen. He was constantly, as his wife said, "bothering" her, even into his eighth decade. One bastard son, Timothy, was at hand, a child that he fathered with a servant called Akinsa. The problem was that Timothy looked exactly like Tolstoy. Even the same white beard, the haggard look and crooked nose, the voice. Only Timothy was something of an idiot. I'm using that term in a literal sense—he was mentally slow, childlike. It haunted Tolstoy to have this son wandering around the house looking like a shadow version of himself.

Swaim: One of the contradictions you mentioned: he believed in poverty and yet he was one of the wealthiest men in Russia.
Parini: He grew up as a privileged member of one of the most elite families in all of Russia. Prince Volkonsky—an ancestor—had been an associate of Peter the Great. It was a noble lineage.

Swaim: But his relationship with his wife, that's extraordinary.
Parini: Sofya was the daughter of a physician to the Tzar. She grew up in the Kremlin itself, in the court circle, and considered it a coup when she

married Tolstoy, the famous young author and nobleman of her time. She expected a life of luxury and privilege as well as intellectual stimulation—she was a very smart, interesting, wise woman. Early on, she realized she was in for a rough ride. He was a tempestuous man. Just before they got married, he thrust his early diaries on her, asking her to read them. He was early thirties. She was only eighteen. It shocked her to see that he'd been sleeping with whores and all sorts of women. He recorded every instance of sexual congress, as he called it; his exploits were far too explicit for her taste. It horrified her that the man she had consented to marry was a rake. Nevertheless, she went through with the marriage. She did, after all, want to be the Countess Tolstoy. I think she was happiest in the early years of their marriage, when he settled into family life, the life of a working author. They moved to his large, ancestral house in Tula province—a beautiful estate, still available to visitors, called Yasnaya Polyana. There Tolstoy wrote *War and Peace, Anna Karenina, Death of Ivan Ilyich*. Many of his greatest works of fiction were written there. But in middle age, he experienced a religious conversion, which he described in his confessions. He saw the light, or a light, and began to preach his own version of Christianity, which was a kind of post-Enlightenment non-supernatural Christianity. He believed Christ was a man like every other man—but a gifted man, inspired by God. As he would, Tolstoy devoted himself to learning biblical Greek, going through the Gospels and editing them, taking out the supernatural bits. He sought a naturalist Christianity, regarding Christ as one of many disciples in a line of prophets going back to Socrates, going back to the Buddha, and so forth. A great teacher. As I said, he himself became a guru; yet he was tortured by his earlier life and present compulsions. The contradictions in his body and brain began to tear him apart. He started doing things like wishing to banish all servants from the household. He had perhaps thirty servants in the house itself. He fervently wished to live more simply. He forged a plan to give away the copyrights on his books to the public. He didn't want to benefit from his royalties—especially royalties on novels, which he considered a decadent form of expression. He had become a puritanical fanatic in his later years. Even worse, he surrounded himself with a group of so-called Tolstoyans—people who believed in his religious and social ideas even more fiercely than he did himself. They tended to push the puritanical streak to its limits. One of his fiercest disciples was Vladimir Chertkov, his publisher and one of my principal speakers in the novel. He was—at least as I imagine him—a dark and tormented figure, one who took the ideas of his master a bit too seriously, too literally. I found his writing rather eerily narrow-minded, even dull. He set up a publishing company and retreat house near Tolstoy called Telyatinki. He and his associates would make regular visits to the Tolstoy estate, joining the throng who gathered there, all hoping for a glimpse of the great man. On any given morning, anywhere from ten to fifty people would appear on Tolstoy's doorstep. As she would, Sofya—she's called Sofya by people in the community, Sonya only by Tolstoy himself; it's a very intimate name, Sonya, in Russian—became increasingly paranoid about Chertkov and ill-at-ease with the Tolstoyans. She was afraid Tolstoy was going to give away their money, leaving her and the children destitute. They'd become accustomed to the privileged lifestyle of Russian aristocrats. Lots of cash was needed to support their trips to Paris, visits to the opera, and for the support of townhouses, droshkies, servants, and so forth. Tolstoy wanted to get out from under all of this extravagance. Eventually, he decided to go on the road and become a kind of wandering ascetic. He actually wished he could live in a monastery. For many years, he planned to be like elderly Buddhists or Hindus. At a certain stage they say it's time to stop clinging to earthly possessions and renounce their family name, property, stations in life, and try to get in touch with a deeper self, with God. That's what Tolstoy longed to do. His readers often wrote to him about the life he led, urging him to live in accordance with his principles. They hoped for perfection in the master. I found one letter from a factory worker in Baku, who wrote saying: "What are you doing? We all believe in your values, but your life embarrasses us." As it would, Tolstoy's daily habits got reported in the press. And Tolstoy was deeply pained by the contradictions in his life. The publicity mill was fairly rudimentary in those days compared to now, but Tolstoy was among the first world celebrities to come from the ranks of literature. Reporters constantly tracked him, described his every move, reported on everything he said. So by October of 1910, he had about had it, so he split. He woke Dr. Dushan Makovitsky, his personal physician, in the middle of the night and said, "Pack up. We're leaving. And don't forget the enema bag!" They saddled the horses, rode off to the train station. Tolstoy hoped that was going to be it. For the next five, ten years—however long he lived—he would be on the road and perhaps wind up in some isolated community, where he'd live anonymously in some little *izba* or hut. It was a dream.

Swaim: We should note that at this point he was, I believe, eighty-two.
Parini: Yes, but in relatively good health: riding his horse every day, energetic, mentally acute—he had an immense correspondence with people from around the world, and he wrote letters, stories, essays until near the

end. He was healthy in mind and body. But the strain of movement defeated him at last, and he didn't survive on the road. He fell ill almost at once. My novel dramatizes what happened: at the end, he lay dying in a train station in a remote part of Russia, and he believed he was dying alone, in the small house of the stationmaster, surrounded by only a handful of close associates, including his beloved daughter, Sasha. He didn't want his wife to discover his whereabouts; but the stationmaster leaked the message out to reporters, and soon journalists arrived from Moscow, St. Petersburg, Paris, London, and Bonn—everybody converged on tiny Astapovo. They formed a make-shift village of tents, with regular press statements delivered by Tolstoy's doctor.

Swaim: Literally a circus.
Parini: It *was* a circus. Hundreds of reporters flocked to the scene, surrounding the stationmaster's house.

Swaim: Old newsreel cameramen?
Parini: That's right. Some of the first Pathé cameramen were there, cranking away. Those films are still available, and I had access to them. They were shown recently on the Discovery Channel. The Countess, of course, rented a first-class train, as she would. It pulled into the station with considerable drama. She and her surviving children and many servants wanted to see Tolstoy. Chertkov tried, with some luck, to protect Tolstoy from this siege. The old man was fairly delirious, but would go in and out of lucidity. He didn't know that Sofya was there. She was never admitted to the little house where he lay dying until the last moment, as he lapsed into a coma. There's a pathetic newsreel of her pounding at the window, begging to be let in before he died, with Chertkov shooing her away.

Swaim: He was certainly a gentleman, despite his puritanical beliefs toward the end. He was gentle and kind.
Parini: One should never lose sight of the fact that Tolstoy was a great man, and that greatness lay in his simplicity, his directness with people, his kindness and gentility. He was a sincere man, too, though driven to a kind of egomania; usually, he kept this in check and was aware of it and felt guilty about it. He was a Christian gentleman, in the best sense of that phrase. I admire him.

Swaim: Chertkov is a very dark character in the novel. Can you elaborate on that?

Parini: He was born into an upper class family and, like many of his class, had been in the army, but there he grew uncomfortable with the Russian system, which he regarded as unjust. So he resigned his commission, becoming a proselytizer for Tolstoyan ideas—a philosophical view that chimed with his own ideas. He was anti-Tzarist, so it wasn't a surprise that they kicked him out of Russia for a lengthy period, during which time he corresponded with Tolstoy. He helped set up a Tolstoy circle in London and to translate Tolstoy's works from Russian into English. When he came back to Russia, he linked up with Tolstoy as before, even though the government looked on their relationship with trepidation. Tolstoy regarded him as his closest friend. But he was a jealous friend, and suspicious of Tolstoy's wife, whom he regarded as an obstacle of sorts. He wished that Tolstoy had never married and could devote himself totally to his political and religious ideas. As you might imagine, Sofya hated Chertkov. They had a deep personality conflict—like oil and water. So the battle between them became one of the pivotal stories in the final year of Tolstoy's life. Chertkov wished to get possession of Tolstoy's will. This document came to represent more than the will itself. It became a symbolic thing, representing the battle for Tolstoy's soul. Chertkov needed to possess Tolstoy. He wanted to own Tolstoy and his ideas and vision. Sofya, of course, wanted Tolstoy for herself, for the family. She was motherly toward the old man, so to speak. She thought of him as a child being duped by these crazy Tolstoyans—especially Chertkov, whom she regarded as self-serving and satanic. A pitched battle developed between the two of them, with various attempts at rapprochement, as obviously Tolstoy was married to Sofya Andreyevna. It wasn't easy for him to leave home. I'm still amazed that he actually did it. It took him until his eighty-second year, after all. He began to think about ending the marriage many years before. It took years to get up the courage to leave. It was an incredibly tortured decision, but it finally did occur, with Chertkov's encouragement.

Swaim: Have you read all of Tolstoy's works?

Parini: There's an awful lot of Tolstoy, and I'm sure I've missed out on some things. The Russian edition of *The Works of Leo Tolstoy* runs to about a hundred volumes. I've certainly read all the major novels and shorter stories and novellas, and I've read most of his letters. I've read his diaries. So I've got a fairly clear picture of Tolstoy's achievement.

Swaim: I would imagine that, as a writer, you might have to know a hundred percent of Tolstoy, but maybe use five percent.

Parini: That's true. You have to do research for anything you write, of course. But when you're writing an historical novel set deeply in the past, you have a lot of work before you. You need to know the details: how the trains work, and were there electric lights in the house. Were there cars on the roads? What social relations obtained between the classes? But you learn to forget most of the things you discover. You keep your eye on the story. Story is everything, and details can get in the way. You must keep the flow of the narrative before you at every moment, avoiding the temptations to stick in the little bits of research. Just because you know something, you don't have to say it. I often dislike big historical novels, like, say, novels by James Michener, where facts are sort of hanging in the soup like bits of fat: little dumplings of knowledge that are indigestible and swirling in the soup. Too much cholesterol there. I try to put my research through a process where it's blended in a kind of artistic Cuisinart. The narrative isn't interrupted. I wanted this book to possess the narrative flow of a thriller. I hope that I managed that. I found it exciting to write. Even though I alternate voices in *The Last Station*, I hope there's narrative momentum.

Swaim: There's no doubt the suspense keeps building. When you start reading a book, you worry a little bit, "Am I going to like this? Am I going to be bored by it?" That's a commitment. So with the first couple of chapters, I wasn't sure who was talking at first.

Parini: It takes a little time to hear the voices, to get a feel for the tone of each speaker. The hope is that soon the reader grows accustomed to each speaker, comes to understand his or her range—tonally, the range of associations.

Swaim: Also, you use the Russian familiar names. I would sometimes have to go back and say, "Now, who are they talking about?" But after a while, the characters gelled. You got to know who was speaking. You could almost tell without even looking at the title of the chapter who was speaking.

Parini: As I wrote, I became familiar with each voice. A particular tone or vocal timbre would haunt me as I worked on a given chapter. I was afraid I'd discourage readers, with the Russian names, and with the fact that so often I begin a story in the middle. My hope was that readers would make the necessary adjustments. That's the work of reading. It's active work, but that is usually the most engaging.

Swaim: I knew nothing about Tolstoy—nothing. Tolstoy is one of these writers everybody claims to have read.
Parini: I think so. Everyone has read Homer, too, and Dante. But few have.

Swaim: And nobody has read Tolstoy! I have yet to meet anybody other than yourself who has really read—and my wife, who is a big Russian reader—she studied Russian at Hunter—who has actually read *War and Peace*.
Parini: It's a classic novel, meaning it's one you put on your shelf for retirement reading. I can imagine these groaning shelves everywhere in the world, with *Madame Bovary*, *The Iliad*, *Germinal*, and *The Brothers Karamazov* waiting for eyes.

Swaim: I also like what you said about making a story instead of writing undigested facts in the way that Michener often does. I read a book by Arthur Hailey not too long ago, and it was not a bad story. But I think the book could have been half as large, and probably twice as good, without being bogged down in all those facts.
Parini: A large segment of the American population thinks that books must be good for them, and they ought to learn something—such as how airplanes work or how hotels are built or whatever. There are better ways of finding out those things. I go to books for a spiritual adventure. I'm interested in the life of the mind and the life of the spirit, and Tolstoy is one of the great aids of all those who wish to live in the spirit.

Swaim: At the same time, this is a historical novel, and it tells you about Tolstoy. I mean, I learned things about Tolstoy—in a very easy, digestible way. I think that's where people really learn history. I mean, they can't go to a history book. We had to do that in grade school and high school. We had to read history books about the Reconstruction era and all of that. But if you really want to find out what happens, what happened in our history, you go to a fiction writer.
Parini: That's true. One of the best ways to learn and remember facts is within a narrative context. If I want to learn about a subject, abstractly, I can look things up. If I should suddenly feel a need to learn something about Czechoslovakia, I can go to the encyclopedia and get a number of facts, and I will probably not remember any of them. But if I read about Czechoslovakia in a novel by Milan Kundera, suddenly I have a narrative context in which to place the facts, an inner sense of what these facts mean to people

in their emotional lives. It's the response to fact that's interesting. Fiction is a wonderful educational tool.

Swaim: Jay Parini, you're a poet. Tell me about your life in poetry.
Parini: Well, I really started off as a poet, and consider myself, primarily, a poet. I was trained as a poet. My first love was poetry. I've written a book on the American poet Theodore Roethke, and I've written three or four books of poetry. I spend a lot of time readings poets.

Swaim: How is one trained as a poet?
Parini: All poets are self-trained. You train as a poet by starting with Chaucer or Beowulf, learning about the traditions of poetry: how lines are shaped, rhythms developed. You learn the actual content of the history of English and European poetry, reading the poetry itself and criticism of poetry. Mainly, you learn to write poetry by writing poems—good, bad, and ugly. You have to discover what poems are made of. So you always are a self-trained poet—you can't be taught poetry. But you can be taught how to train yourself. You can be helped in training yourself. I spent many years in universities. I studied for seven years at the University of St. Andrews in Scotland, for example, where I had marvelous teachers, a few of them poets themselves, who worked with me and helped me learn the rudiments of verse, how to think in metaphors, how to use language, to create images, how to make poems that convey emotion, that build and reach a climax. I learned how to make my own burdens into language, turn them into poems. My poetry, I hope, is a language that's somehow adequate to my own experience, that embodies it as well as reflects it, and, hopefully, that transforms it. So for me poetry is a daily, spiritual activity. Fiction is simply an extension of my poetry. I found my poems getting longer and longer, moving toward narrative. At a certain point, I moved into fiction to experience the narrative sweep of novels, as a writer. I've come to love writing novels as an adjunct to my poetry. There's no separation between fiction and poetry in my writing life. It's all language, and it's all part of the same ongoing contextualizing of my life and language, a creating of life, my imaginative life, in language. Increasingly, I spend more time on fiction, but that's because it takes more time. I find that I'm able to bring a lot of the same concerns that led me to write poetry into the making of fiction.

Swaim: Of course, writing fiction is going to bring you a much wider audience.

Parini: It's shocking, in fact. I've written books of poems published by publishers like Random House and Henry Holt, and one barely gets a handful of readers for poetry—even with a major publisher. I write a novel like *The Last Station*, and suddenly it's in its fourth printing, on the front page of the *New York Times Book Review*. I'm not sure that fiction deserves the kind of attention it sometimes gets. I suppose there is simply a craving for narrative, and novels satisfy that craving—good novels, that is.

Swaim: How does one get a poem published? I'm an amateur poet myself. I've sent out hundreds of poems, and I have yet to see one published. They all come back.

Parini: The market for poetry is terrible. It matches the audience for poetry.

Swaim: Even the little magazines seem to be run by a clique of people.

Parini: That's the problem. The poetry world is a very small, clique-ish world. The main audience for poetry is other poets. There is a lot of power-brokering within this absurdly small group. The poetry world is comical in some ways, with its petty arguments and trends and "schools." That's why I feel relieved to be in the world of fiction, where you're not subjected quite so brutally to literary cliques of the kind that tend to dominate in the field of poetry.

Swaim: Why don't we have these big, sprawling narrative poems that—like Longfellow used to write anymore?

Parini: Readers nowadays have a small attention span. Poetry's a very concentrated form, and to, say, read a long, dense narrative poem like *The Divine Comedy* requires an immense amount of concentration and patience. You have to understand the context, grow familiar with the range of allusion. The effort is worth it; but it remains an effort.

Swaim: But poetry could be accessible, like "By the shores of Gitchy Goomey . . . "—I'm referring to *Hiawatha*. These Longfellow poems are accessible, but they're not published now. Maybe they're not written. I've been doing a lot of reading about Ambrose Bierce during his heyday in the late 1800s, early 1900s—newspapers published his poems. Edward Markham was one of Bierce's protégés. He wrote a very famous poem that appeared in a newspaper in San Francisco and was republished all over the United States. This doesn't happen anymore. These were narrative poems. They told stories.

Parini: That's right. In fact, there have been some long narrative poems written in the last couple of decades that are good. I'm thinking of James Merrill's *The Changing Light at Sandover*, and one or two other poems. W. H. Auden, several decades ago, wrote some long and successful poems, such as *Letter to Lord Byron* or *The Sea and the Mirror*. Robert Lowell wrote *The Mills of the Kavanaughs*. Ginsburg wrote *Howl*, which has a certain notoriety. But narrative poems haven't had a wide audience in our time, that's true. This is an age of short confessional lyrics, for the most part.

Swaim: I tried to read Merrill's book. I didn't understand a word.
Parini: It's elliptical and complex and postmodern. Perhaps a more accessible narrative poem for you would be Robert Penn Warren's *Chief Joseph of the Nez Perce*, a poem about the great Indian hero. Or *Audubon: A Vision*, another one of Warren's fine books.

Swaim: Where did you go to college?
Parini: Lafayette College, then St. Andrews. I went off to Scotland on my junior year abroad, and pretty much stayed. I did a Ph.D. in English. I started to write poems seriously, novels, too, in Scotland. I never even tried to publish my first couple of novels. I thought of it as a practice work. I came back to teach in 1975, when I got a job as a young poet at Dartmouth College in New Hampshire. It was a lucky stroke. I had published my first book of poems in Scotland, in 1972, and I had a lot of essays in print. In my twenties, I had poems published in the *New Yorker* and the *Atlantic*. Random House took my first mature collection of poems, *Anthracite Country*, which got fairly wide notice for a book of poems. While at Dartmouth, my first published novel appeared from Atlantic-Little Brown. Since then, I've pretty much evenly divided my time between poetry and fiction, with miscellaneous reviews and criticism on the side.

Swaim: Of course, you teach as well.
Parini: Yes, and I have a family. So it's a busy life, but, I hope, an integrated life. I try to keep my days calm enough so that all of the things I'm interested in doing have a place, and the different pieces of my life inform all the other pieces. A balanced life seems important.

Swaim: Do you have a place where you can go hide and work?
Parini: We live in a beautiful but old and dilapidated farmhouse. It used to be the hired hand's lodging for the Morgan Horse Farm, outside of Middlebury, Vermont. When we bought the place, it was a rundown sheep farm.

There were dead sheep lying in the field. The porch was falling off, the foundation was askew. Mice nested in every little cranny and nook—and there were an awful lot of crannies and nooks. We've slowly been restoring the house, very slowly; as soon as we restore one bit, another bit falls down. But we've got isolation on our little hilltop. We have a marvelous view of the Green Mountains, with a field of horses outside. We have woods to walk in, streams to observe, a pond nearby. And, of course, Lake Champlain isn't far away.

Swaim: I think Tolstoy would have liked this place.
Parini: It's very Tolstoyan.

Swaim: How do you find the time to do this work?
Parini: The mornings are my special time. I've always written in the morning—from eight o'clock until twelve, noon, or one. That's my sacred time, and unless I'm traveling, I write—six or seven days a week. It's amazing how much you can get done in three or four hours, if you do it every day of your life. I work especially well when I've got something in motion: a book with a narrative arc. That keeps me moving. I once had a tip from John Updike: write two pages a day. I try to do that, when I'm working on prose. If I manage four pages or five, I'm on a hot streak. With poetry, of course, it's very different. A poem can take minutes to write, or decades.

Swaim: The self-discipline . . . I just wonder how many people have that discipline to be able to sit down, alone, in a room, and work like that. I have a feeling most people can't.
Parini: I was lucky to be given an even temperament. I get agitated at times, of course. Who doesn't? And sometimes I have a hard time writing. But usually, I find something to work on. I can always lower my standards, as they say; the writing will flow. I go to my desk eagerly most days, which is a lucky thing. I wake up with work in my head. It's rarely a chore to make my way to my desk.

Swaim: Back to the poems. There's—do you have a specific theme, or approach, with regard to your poetry?
Parini: I stay away from fashion. My poems live within the traditions of English and American verse. I try to write plainly, with a kind of sensuous, concrete approach—very imagistic. I bring ideas in my poetry whenever I have one, as well as an image. One of the obsessions of modernist poetry

was that one should never bring ideas into verse. William Carlos Williams said, "No ideas, but in things." Yet I'm a great fan of discursive poetry, too. So in my most recent book, as in *Town Life*, I have some long, essayistic poems in which I talk about ideas, Plato, and so forth. There's a long sequence on reading Emerson. But for the most part, my poems are simple, concrete and sensuous, and they're quite lyrical. I'm interested in the music of language. I love Frost, Heaney, and poets in that particular vein, with a realistic edge, place-centered. Yet I'm drawn to the linguistic bravado of Wallace Stevens, his philosophical range.

Swaim: What about this confessional mode of poetry that Robert Lowell used to specialize in?

Parini: A fair portion of my poetry is autobiographical, but it's not confessional. The confessional mode that Lowell, Berryman, Plath, and company indulged in was self-indulgent in many ways. I don't like Lowell as much in his more self-indulgent vein. I prefer "The Quaker Graveyard at Nantucket." I especially disliked Berryman in his self-indulgent mode. I prefer Robert Frost in his oblique autobiographical poems, where he's able to move outside himself to find a metaphor in which to pour himself, to study life through metaphor; education by metaphor, he called it. "After Apple-Picking" is almost a perfect poem in that regard. The picking of apples is analogous to the possibilities for poetry, for good things in life. So many apples to "cherish in hand," and I think poems are like that. We cherish the images, the language itself. We explore the possibilities for expression. That's what I'm trying to do, in any case. Poets live in language, pushing its boundaries, finding its deeper resonances.

Interview with Chris Bohjalian

Chris Bohjalian / 1997

From the *Boston Globe* (October 26, 1997), 17:2. Reprinted by permission. Chris Bohjalian is the author of sixteen books, including *The Light in the Ruins*, *The Sandcastle Girls*, and *Midwives*.

Poet, novelist, and bespectacled English professor Jay Parini was sitting beside football great Harvey Martin, an All-Pro defensive lineman. Martin had just finished regaling an audience of four hundred with his story about the time he had chewed off a part of an opposing player's ear. It was 1986, and the two were sharing the dais at an "authors' dinner" in Pittsburgh. Parini had been invited because his lyric coming-of-age novel, *The Patch Boys*, was set in Pennsylvania's anthracite country. Martin was touring on behalf of his autobiography, *Texas Thunder: My Eleven Years with the Dallas Cowboys*. After the two men spoke, a long line formed before the tall piles of Martin's book, as most of the audience queued up to buy copies. Parini thought he was going to be completely alone, until one intrepid soul finally positioned himself before Parini and his high stack of *The Patch Boys*.

"You know, I liked you better when you played for the Steelers," the fellow remarked, as he thumbed abstractedly through the novel.

Parini smiles when he tells the story and then sits forward on the couch in the living room of his 1850 Vermont farmhouse. "As funny as it was that my one fan was confused, that wasn't even the best part of the night," he recalls. "When the evening was over, Harvey Martin asked me—and he was completely serious—'Who wrote your book?'"

Jay Parini was thirty-eight that night in Pittsburgh. He's now flirting with fifty. In the decade in between, he has published three more novels, a poetry collection, a poetry textbook, and a biography of John Steinbeck. He has also edited or coedited eleven anthologies of other people's poems and essays.

Altogether, in the last two decades, his name has appeared on the cover of twenty-two books, almost all of them critically acclaimed. Right now, he is in the midst of a particularly prolific period: Including his most recent novel, *Benjamin's Crossing*, published last May, and his long-awaited biography of Robert Frost, which will be published next fall, he will have seven new books published in an eighteen-month period. And when he's not writing, he's teaching. He's the Axinn Professor of English at Middlebury College.

Jay Parini just might be the hardest-working writer you've never heard of. Within the literary community, however, Parini is a household name. His friend Erica Jong asked him to help her choose which poems to keep and which ones to discard from her most recent collection. His friendship with Ann Beattie began when she wrote him a fan letter after reading one of his poems twenty years ago in the *New Yorker*. And Gore Vidal—aloof, sardonic, unapproachable Gore Vidal—called Parini's novel about Leo Tolstoy's final days, *The Last Station*, "easily one of the best historical novels written in the last twenty years."

Parini reviews books frequently for the *Boston Globe* and the *New York Times*, he writes academic explorations of literary theory for the *Hudson Review*, and he edited both the *Columbia Anthology of American Poetry* and the *Columbia History of American Poetry*.

Yet of Parini's twenty-two books as author, editor, or coeditor, only his 1995 biography of John Steinbeck has ever sold as many as 15,000 copies. Even *The Last Station*, which received a glowing review in 1990 on the front page of the *New York Times Book Review*, sold barely 12,000 copies in cloth.

Undoubtedly, his sales figures reflect his choice of topics. *Benjamin's Crossing*, for example, is a novel about the German-Jewish literary critic and philosopher Walter Benjamin and his wild attempt to cross the Pyrenees Mountains into Spain in 1940, after Paris fell to the Nazis. And though the book is in part a gripping adventure tale, the fact remains that a novel about an obscure Frankfurt-school intellectual is a hard sell in this country.

"If any other writer, with the exception, perhaps, of Susan Sontag, had come to me with the idea for a novel about Walter Benjamin, I would have discouraged it," says Allen Peacock, Parini's editor at Henry Holt and Company. "But Jay is such a classically intuitive biographer and storyteller that I knew he would do the story justice."

Parini has chosen slightly more esoteric—and considerably less marketable—subject matter for each novel. In 1992, before *Benjamin's Crossing*, he wrote *Bay of Arrows*, a rich but complex exploration of the myth of Christopher Columbus, juxtaposing the story of the fifteenth-century explorer with that of a self-absorbed twentieth-century English professor. Before that, in

1990, he imagined the anarchy that existed inside the Tolstoy estate at the end of the great writer's life.

In 1986, he wrote his deeply moving story of a boy growing up in coal country in 1925, *The Patch Boys*. And close to two decades ago, as a young assistant professor at Dartmouth College, he published *The Love Run*, a page-turner about a pair of working-class New Hampshire youths who kidnap the wealthy, entitled, and desperately libidinous Dartmouth undergraduate Maisie Danston.

While the premise of his first book was undeniably commercial, Parini didn't take the project particularly seriously. During the summer that he was writing the novel, his wife—short-story writer and literary critic Devon Jersild—and Scottish poet Alastair Reid, who was visiting them at the time, took the liberty of adding whole paragraphs to the manuscript when they'd find a page sitting in the typewriter.

Certainly, most writers interested in turning material from the lives of Benjamin and Tolstoy into novels would find it difficult to get even one publisher interested in their work, yet Parini has books under contract with four publishers. In the next year alone, each publisher will be releasing at least one title with Parini's name on the cover.

This week, University Press of New England will publish *Beyond the Godfather*, a group of essays by Italian-American writers on the Italian-American experience, coedited by Parini with A. Kenneth Ciongoli, the president of the National Italian American Foundation. In February, Columbia University Press will publish the first collection of Parini's essays, *Some Necessary Angels*. In April, Henry Holt will publish Parini's fourth collection of poetry, *House of Days*. And late next year, W. W. Norton will publish *The Norton Anthology of American Autobiography*, which Parini is editing.

None of these books, however, will have large print runs: *Beyond the Godfather*, for example, had a 4,000-copy first printing, and the print run for *Some Necessary Angels* will be only about 5,000. A new novel from popular fiction writers Michael Crichton or John Grisham will sell that many copies in a day.

But the irony in the eyes of many of his fellow writers and friends is that if more readers gave Parini's work a chance, they'd be hooked. If anyone, in their opinion, can make people like Tolstoy and Benjamin interesting and accessible, it's Jay Parini. Parini doesn't look like a man approaching fifty, especially when he's hoisting his three-year-old son, Leo, into his arms or playing basketball at the college gym—his exercise three days a week. His face seems to have no more wrinkles today than it did when he was forty, and though he is absolutely bald, he had already lost most of his hair by his late thirties. The face that peers out at readers from the 1997 *Benjamin's Crossing* doesn't look any different from the one smiling at readers on the back of his eleven-year-old novel, *The Patch Boys*.

"When I entertain notions of the lives I might have had, in one of those lives I write best-selling novels," he says, placing his glass of iced tea on a picnic table in his front yard, on a warm day in September. Across the street is one of the pastures of the Morgan Horse Farm, and it's common for there to be fifty horses in the field. In the distance is Mount Abraham, one of a handful of peaks in Vermont taller than 4,000 feet. "I would have tried to train myself to be a Dick Francis or a John Le Carre," he continues. "I'd be very rich now; I'd have a yacht. But I also wouldn't have the satisfactions with my life that I have. I wouldn't be happy."

There is, of course, a wide middle ground in publishing between the astonishing commercial success of a Dick Francis and the modest sales of a Jay Parini. Writers like Cathie Pelletier (*Beaming Sonny Home*), Frederick Busch (*Girls*), and Elizabeth McCracken (*A Giant's House*) can be expected to sell 20,000 to 30,000 copies.

But, so far, none of Parini's books have broken out. None of his novels have generated what publishers call a "buzz" among bookstores and their customers, none of them have generated the early word of mouth that this summer propelled first novels from Charles Frazier (*Cold Mountain*) and Arundhati Roy (*The God of Small Things*) onto bestseller lists.

And editors, publicists, and agents agree: Buzz is essential. Parini's novels come from Henry Holt, a large, distinguished New York publisher, and Holt works hard on Parini's behalf. It doesn't market his books as aggressively as, for example, it does those from its best-selling mystery author, Sue Grafton, but it covers all the basics: Holt sends "prepublication" paperback galleys to bookstores, it schedules book signings, and Holt publicists make sure that book editors and critics receive the novels for review. More important, Holt gets Parini's books shelf space in the crowded "New Fiction" sections of bookstores when the novels are first released.

Certainly, Parini's predilection for novels about esoteric or iconic historical figures suggests that, if commercial success is his goal, he's his own worst enemy. And his wide range of writing—fiction, poetry, biography, criticism, and personal essay—also makes him a hard sell. "One of the problems is that Jay has written in so many different fields that he can't be classified—and the market likes to classify things: Novelist. Poet. Critic. But he's that thing we call a 'man of letters,'" says writer Sam Pickering, a friend of Parini's since they were professors at Dartmouth, who's now teaching at the University of Connecticut.

But perhaps more important, there is a self-fulfilling nature to publishing today. *M Is for Malice*, Sue Grafton's 1996 Kinsey Millhone mystery, had a reported first printing fifty times larger than that of *Benjamin's Crossing*: 500,000 copies. When a publisher prints a half-million copies of a novel, it has made a sizable investment that it must try to recoup. It will spend whatever it can to try to turn a profit.

And when retailers hear that a novel has a half-million-copy first printing, they're bound to notice. Even the 40,000-copy first printing of *Cold Mountain* caused much of the publishing community to sit up and take note, since it was for a first novel from an unknown writer. The buzz around *Cold Mountain*—a beautiful and literary Civil War saga—grew especially loud when word spread before publication that paperback rights may have gone for as much as $300,000.

None of Parini's novels have had the large printings or hefty paperback sales that trigger a commercial rumble in this country. Parini actually has a larger following overseas. His biography of John Steinbeck became the No. 4 bestseller in England, and his British and German publishers are planning hefty first printings of *Benjamin's Crossing*.

"It's like anything else: Publishing wants a sure thing," says John Mutter, an executive editor at *Publishers Weekly*, the industry's weekly magazine. "And, these days, there's a real pressure on the large houses to be profitable. They want titles with relatively little risk, vs. well-written literary fiction." On the fifth day of the August 1997 Bread Loaf Writers' Conference, in Ripton, Vermont, the grass is tall in the meadows surrounding the small campus, and the leaves on the hillsides have just started to turn. Parini is in high spirits, chuckling because a newspaper article he has just read suggests that publishers are abandoning the "mid-list novelist"—those novelists whose books sell fewer than 15,000 copies.

"Look at this," he says, waving the article as he rises from an Adirondack chair. "I'm an endangered species." Parini is a faculty member at Bread Loaf, helping some of the 225 aspiring writers who have spent $1,700 to come here for ten days to learn more about the craft and to have their work critiqued by professionals.

Parini can afford to laugh at the newspaper article, because he isn't really in danger of losing a publisher. Nevertheless, he freely admits that he is occasionally disappointed by the notion that he does not have a larger audience outside of this country's small, insular literary community. "There's always the frustration of being a writer in a world that doesn't care about writing—or at least about the kinds of books that I like to write," he says. "Ideally, I believe that my Tolstoy novel or my Benjamin novel should have as many readers as a John Grisham novel, but it's obviously not going to happen."

Nevertheless, Parini's work is marked, in part, by a good-natured wit, and this—along with the quality of his prose—has many of his peers convinced that he is capable of writing not merely literary fiction, but literary fiction that may one day be hit by commercial lightning. "Jay's a little eccentric, and that's a real plus in my mind," says Ann Beattie. "He doesn't write musty history books. He writes books that reflect a modern sensibility and that address issues that matter right now. His books are relevant and readable."

His humor and irreverence are apparent even when he's exploring the most arcane subjects. In an essay in *Some Necessary Angels* in which he addresses the sheer unreadability of most literary criticism, he asks, "What do you get when you cross a deconstructionist with a mafioso? Answer: An offer you can't understand." In another essay in which he's examining the relationship between fact and fiction, especially as it relates to biography, there is this:

"Not long after I began my research on the Steinbeck biography, my subject's widow, Elaine Steinbeck, told me that she had had a dream in which Steinbeck was sitting in heaven at dinner beside Leo Tolstoy. The famous American novelist told the great Russian writer that Jay Parini was about to write his biography. 'Good luck, old man,' Tolstoy exclaimed. 'Have you seen what he did to me?'"

And while his most recent novel, *Benjamin's Crossing*, is certainly filled with the kind of philosophical minutia that mattered to Walter Benjamin, Parini never lets the reader lose sight of the fact that his forty-eight-year-old intellectual hero must evade Nazis, collaborators, and border guards while performing what is for him the incredibly arduous task of crossing the Pyrenees into Spain.

For Parini, this was an important part of his design for the book. "I once asked Gore Vidal if you could have two characters in a novel discuss Kierkegaard for twelve pages without losing the reader, and he said, 'You can if they're sitting in a railway car, and the reader knows there's a bomb under the seat.' In *Benjamin's Crossing*, my hope is that the Nazis are that bomb," Parini says.

This recent novel, like most of Parini's work, was reviewed widely and usually admired. In the *New York Times Book Review*, Robert Grudin concluded, "*Benjamin's Crossing* is not only a humane book, it is also a lively one." Marcie Hershman wrote in the *Boston Sunday Globe* that Benjamin himself would have been pleased by the structure of Parini's book and by the way "Benjamin's flight shares equal weight with a rendering of his intellectual—and intellectualized—relationships." Yet despite the frequent and favorable reviews, Henry Holt sold only about 10,000 copies of the novel. Because Parini is so productive, there are many writers who assume that writing must be effortless for him. It's not.

On a typical weekday this fall, he will be awake at 6:30 a.m. to help get his two older sons off to school: In addition to three-year-old Leo, he and Devon have fifteen-year-old Will and twelve-year-old Oliver. Parini usually will be in his study, in what used to be the basement of the farmhouse, by 8 a.m., where he will write until early afternoon or later. Then he will go to the college, where he teaches, advises students, or attends department and faculty meetings.

Tuesdays and Thursdays are particularly long days. From 3 p.m. until 4:20, he will teach the college's freshman seminar on the language of poetry, and then, from 4:30 until 6 o'clock, he will have open office hours for his students. At 6:15, he will pick up his oldest son at football practice at the nearby public high school, have dinner with his family until 7:15, and then return to the college, where he will teach the senior seminar on modern poetry from 7:30 to 10:30. "There's always a demand for teachers who will teach evening classes, and I'm happy to do that, to keep my mornings free to write," he says.

And though Parini admits that teaching occasionally gets in the way of writing, he says he can't imagine not teaching. "Teaching is an opportunity for me to play the role with younger writers that older writers have played with me," he says. For his forthcoming collection, he has written a special essay about the older writers whose friendship and counsel have influenced him most.

"The idea of mentors has always meant a great deal to me, because I come from a nonliterary background," Parini says. "From the beginning, I was desperate to find people who would be models for how to live my life as a writer."

Parini describes his family as "intimate, but not literary." He grew up in Scranton, Pennsylvania, where his father was an insurance salesman who became a Baptist minister, and his mother was a housewife. Neither of his parents went to college. Along with his younger sister, Dorrie, the Parinis were a "very cozy, happy postwar family."

Originally, Parini went to Lafayette College, in Easton, Pennsylvania, but in 1968, after two years there, he decided to spend his junior year abroad at

St. Andrews University, in Scotland. He would remain there until 1975, earning his doctorate in English literature.

At St. Andrews, he also met the man he considers his first mentor, Alastair Reid. There would be long periods when almost every day he would pedal his bicycle to Reid's cottage and share with the older writer a poem he'd just written. Reid would go through it line by line, crossing out words and adding new ones, while Parini nervously watched.

"I modeled myself as a teacher after him, too," Parini says. "He really has that combination of sternness and clarity, that British no-nonsense. But it's always clear that he wants to help you."

Yet Reid is only one of easily a half-dozen writers whom Parini credits with helping him to discover his own voice and for instilling in him the discipline it takes to be a writer. And just as these writers were generous with their time, now he is unselfish with the younger writers he sees at Middlebury and Bread Loaf, who send him their manuscripts to read long after they've graduated. On a wall near Parini's desk in his study are twelve cubbyholes in four rows of three. Each of the cubbyholes is perhaps a foot square, and each is filled with spiral notebooks, bound manuscripts, and thick stacks of stapled papers.

"Each of those cubbies is for a different project," Parini explains. These days, that means that one cubby is for *House of Days*, his forthcoming collection of poems; another is for *The Norton Anthology of American Autobiography*. One is filled with the different drafts of *Benjamin's Crossing*, a book he wrote first in longhand at bistros and in libraries in Paris.

The fact that Parini actually needs twelve square feet of cubbyholes for what he calls his "projects" is a literal illustration of the breadth of his interests. He acknowledges that his work ranges far and wide, but he wouldn't have it any other way.

"I hope my brain isn't compartmentalized to the degree that one thing doesn't always impinge upon another," he says. "That's the secret to my writing life. Everything impinges. I have no doubt that my Walter Benjamin novel arose out of my interest in literary theory. And poetry has certainly influenced my fiction. It's made my prose more imagistic. Sentence for sentence, I think my fiction is better because I've learned about rhythm and meter."

And while the poetic rhythm and meter that mark much of Parini's fiction may never make him a best-selling novelist—or, perhaps, as large a draw as a football player who's chewed human flesh—they will always be appreciated by that devoted circle of readers who have discovered his work.

Jay Parini Interview:
Robert Frost: A Life

Brian Lamb / 1999

Transcribed from C-SPAN's *Booknotes* interview with Jay Parini, which was taped on August 3, 1999, and aired on September 12, 1999. Copyright © 1999 by C-SPAN. http://www
.booknotes.org/Watch/151354-1/Jay+Parini.aspx.

BRIAN LAMB, HOST: Jay Parini, author of *Robert Frost: A Life.* How much had been written about him in biography form before you started.

JAY PARINI: I started on this book a long time ago, almost twenty-five years ago to date when I actually got the idea and began doing some research on Frost in the Dartmouth library, where they had a lot of his papers, including letters and notebooks. But there's been a lot written about Robert Frost. A massive three-volume biography by Lawrence Thompson came out in the late sixties and seventies, and there are countless other lives of Frost— three or four books about him from the late fifties and sixties. So it's not as though Frost hasn't been done before. The question comes, of course: Why bother, given the fact that so much is written about him?

LAMB: What is the story about Thompson?

PARINI: It's important, first, to notice that Frost attracted biographers from the beginning. But the first biographers only wanted to say what a great old fellow Frost was, to romanticize him. The early biographies were puff pieces, magazine profiles blown up into books. Thompson was picked by Frost as the official biographer in 1942 because they became friends. Thompson knew Frost well until the poet's death in 1963. Thompson was a presence in Frost's life and had a romantic involvement with Kay Morrison, Frost's secretary.

LAMB: You suggest in your book, though, that Frost hated him, didn't like him.

PARINI: He came to despise him in a curious way. Thompson was fawning and—and prying; he didn't like Frost's attentions to Kay Morrison. Thompson was attracted to Kay as well. It grew very complicated, and personal issues intervened. By the end of his life, Frost said to several of his friends, "Please save me from Larry. This is going to be a vindictive biography." But Frost died giving full permission to Thompson to do this book, what amounts to a character assassination, which isn't to say it's not a solidly researched book. It does have an amazing amount of good material, basic evidence. More valuable than the actual biography—for my purposes—was the large file of notes Thompson took through his twenty years of working on the book. This was a gold mine for me. Thompson's notes are in the University of Virginia Library. Often the notes seemed at odds with what he finally wrote in the biography. Thompson's biography, like all biographies, is a work of fiction. It's a shaped series of facts with a particular spin on it. There's no biography that is objective, but Thompson's is particularly unobjective. It has this negative spin, which taints it. A biographer must love his subject.

LAMB: Who was Kay Morrison?

PARINI: A young and beautiful woman whom Frost first met in the twenties, when she was a student at Bryn Mawr. He reconnected with her later, after she had married a man who taught at Harvard and directed the English school at Bread Loaf in Vermont, where Frost spent his summers. After the death of his wife, Elinor, in 1938, Kay became Frost's lover, perhaps, then his devoted secretary, and finally his press agent and keeper of the flame. She took on many roles. From 1938 until his death in 1963, Kay was rarely far from Frost. Her husband, Ted Morrison, remained close. This was—not sexually—a kind of *ménage a trois* and very strange in some ways. The Morrison couple kept Frost afloat through difficult years and made it possible for him to play the role of great American bard in the fifties and early sixties, when he was in huge demand as a public speaker.

LAMB: How many Pulitzer Prizes did he win?

PARINI: Four, which is a record—four Pulitzer Prizes for poetry, beginning in 1923 with *New Hampshire* right on through *West-Running Brook*, and so forth, up through *A Witness Tree*. He won a Pulitzer for many of his major books after *New Hampshire*. Quite a record. He was not a prophet without honor in his own country. Just the opposite.

LAMB: What makes Frost's poetry special?

PARINI: The sound of it, so grainy and idiomatic, with a formal under-tow. Frost understood that working within metrical form allowed a poet's voice to play across the formal beat. He cultivated the speaking voice. He understood that poetry was essentially the difference between that abstract form—in pentameter, the five fence posts sticking up—and the way you lay the silk blanket of voice over those posts: the casual or speaking voice, which works against the rigid meter. Think of that delightful opening line of "Mending Wall." "Something there is that doesn't love a wall / That sends the frozen groundswell under it / And spills the upper boulders in the sun." If you read it very abstractly, emphasizing the iambic foot, with its unrelenting *ta-tum, ta-dum*, it would sound crazy, unnatural. Nobody talks like that. But then you lay that lovely blanket of vernacular speech over it, the music of the line emerges in the cadence of the voice. In poem after poem, Frost kept the rigidity of the meter but nevertheless got the language to flow memorably and concretely and beautifully. In "Stopping by Woods," for instance, he creates such a lovely and haunting cadence: "Whose woods these are, I think I know. / His house is in the village, though. / He will not see me stopping here / To watch his woods fill up with snow." Everything is natural and easy-sounding; but it's not easy to write like that. Such memorable phrasing occurs: "The woods are lovely, dark and deep." You can't forget that. It's language made permanent. As Ezra Pound once said, "Poetry is news that stays news." And this is always news. "The woods are lovely, dark and deep, / But I have promises to keep / And miles to go before I sleep. / And miles to go before I sleep." Once you've heard that stanza, it transforms your life because it's language like a deep spring that you can always revisit for refreshment. I've read these poems over thirty years, thousands of times. The poetry always makes my skin prickle. This is news that stays news.

LAMB: You mentioned Ezra Pound, and as you know, that was a very political thing in Robert Frost's life. He was out here at St. Elizabeths Mental Hospital . . . Go to that point, because all kinds of names of people we recognize were involved in Frost trying to get Ezra Pound out of that mental hospital.

PARINI: It's a very strange episode in Frost's life. He was a very unpolitical man. I won't even say apolitical. He was actively against politics in some ways. Having been tried and convicted of treason for his associations with Mussolini and making radio broadcasts on his behalf, Pound was put in St. Elizabeths Hospital. Pound was indeed a crazy fellow and a traitor as well. Frost was one of many writers—Hemingway, T. S. Eliot, Robert Lowell—involved in trying to spring "Old Ez," as they called him, from the hospital, from confinement. But Frost was the point man because he knew President Eisenhower. He had met some key people in the Eisenhower Administration. And it took somebody with ties to the White House, someone admired by Eisenhower and Dulles and Sherman Adams, to get Pound released and deported. They sent him back to Italy.

LAMB: Sherman Adams was the chief of staff to President Eisenhower, but what was the connection there?
PARINI: Adams was an admirer of Frost, loved his poetry and had met him up in New England, in New Hampshire. Adams had been governor of New Hampshire.

LAMB: But on the page and—or the two pages when you're talking about Ezra Pound—but first of all, who is he?
PARINI: One of the founding poets and thinkers of modernism, an American poet who moved to London in the early part of the century, befriended T. S. Eliot and Frost. Later, in Paris, he was close to James Joyce, Hemingway, and Gertrude Stein. And he supported, even systematized, the aesthetics of the modernist movement in poetry. He was the—sort of the ringmaster of modernism in literature. And he had been very kind to Robert Frost at the beginning of his career, helping him to get published. When Frost, totally unknown, aged thirty-eight, sailed to Britain with no books to his credit, no money in his pocket, with a young family and nothing but the hope of a song in his pocket, he met Ezra Pound, who took him up, promoted him, helped him get his books into print, reviewed his first books of poetry, not once but three times. As well he should, Frost felt forever an indebtedness to Pound.

LAMB: On this page you have—where you start to talk about Mr. Frost's attempt to get him out of St. Elizabeths, you say Frost signed a letter, joining Archibald MacLeish in Washington on June 19, 1957, for a meeting at the office of Deputy Attorney General William P. Rogers, who went on to be Secretary of State. Who was MacLeish?
PARINI: Another young poet and playwright that Pound helped in Paris in the twenties. MacLeish was a lawyer and went on to become a minor figure in the Roosevelt Administration. He was a leading Democrat, one of the few poets I can think of who moved easily in the worlds of literature and politics. And MacLeish was an old friend—and sometimes an enemy—of Robert Frost.

LAMB: You mention that Frost didn't like MacLeish.

PARINI: He considered him a third-rate poet, and he didn't care for his liberalism. Frost usually hated liberals. He saw MacLeish as a New Deal Democrat. If Frost had any politics at all, he was a fierce independent, believing in individualism. He was a libertarian in his way. One of his best poems is "Provide, Provide," and it ends, "Better to go down dignified / With boughten friendship at your side / Than none at all. Provide. Provide." And whenever he read that poem, he would say to the audience when he finished, "And if you don't provide for yourself, somebody else is going to provide for you, and you might not like it." He identified MacLeish with that group of urban liberals whom he rather despised.

LAMB: On the subject of Ezra Pound, there's T. S. Eliot, too. What was his relationship to him?

PARINI: Eliot also owed much of his early success to Pound's editing of "The Waste Land." Eliot gave this unwieldy manuscript to Pound, a long poem written while Eliot was recovering from a nervous breakdown in Switzerland. Pound red-penciled it, changing words around, crossing out passages, forging links. Eliot rightly felt that he owed a great deal of his success as a poet to Pound's encouragement, his editing and friendship.

LAMB: You quote Pound as saying—after Frost got him out of St. Elizabeths, as saying, "He ain't been in much of a hurry." And then you say, "When he boarded a liner for Genoa, in New York, he reportedly gave the fascist salute."

PARINI: That might be apocryphal, but what's often said of Ezra Pound is that as the ship was peeling out of the harbor, he put up his hand in a Nazi salute. It's possible, as Pound was deranged. His late sequence of volumes, *The Cantos*, offers a testament to his madness, even though passages of extraordinary beauty shimmer throughout this massive, fragmentary, allusive poem. But the beauty seems random and distant, like lightning over distant mountains.

LAMB: You say, though, that Frost didn't like T. S. Eliot.

PARINI: He thought he was full of humbug and didn't like the way he wore his learning on his shirt-sleeves. He thought that "The Waste Land" was pretentious. I personally regard it as a very great and original poem, but it's a patchwork of quotations from other writers. He quotes an opera by Wagner and pieces of the Upanishads, the religious poetry of India. He quotes bits and pieces of Rimbaud, Verlaine. He quotes oddments of world literature in several languages. Toward the end of the sequence, Eliot writes: "These fragments I have shored against my ruins." These fragments of literature rattled around in his brain as he tried to sustain himself in the broken world of the early twentieth century, the waste land that the world at the Great War had become. But Frost came from a different aesthetic. "The Waste Land" and Eliot's other poetry seemed willfully obscure to him. Remember that Frost was himself a very learned man. He was trained in Latin. He read the *Aeneid*, Catullus, the major Latin poets—all in the original, and right to the end of his life. But he wore his learning very, very lightly.

LAMB: You say he died in 1963, the same year that Jack Kennedy was shot. What was his relationship to President Kennedy?

PARINI: Well, Frost was really the court poet of the Eisenhower Administration. In comes Kennedy, and the first thing that happens is he chooses Frost to read at the inauguration. Soon he became the court poet of the Kennedy Administration. It was Steward Udall, a man who would become Secretary of the Interior, who suggested that Frost read at the inauguration. Kennedy's first response in a memo back to Udall was, "What? That old scene-stealer? They'll forget that I've just been elected president and that's all they'll talk about in the papers the next day," and that really happened. Frost came onto the stage on a bitterly cold day, without a hat, looking very much the part of the ancient wise poet. He was well into his eighties by then, with a face that would have looked good on Mount Rushmore. He couldn't read his poem because of the sun glaring on the sheet. Lyndon Johnson tried to help by shading the podium with his hat. Frost soon brushed him aside and, rather dramatically, recited "The Gift Outright." He made it seem like he pulled it from the recesses of memory with great difficulty; but it wasn't as though he hadn't recited the poem a thousand times before on stage. He was an old ham.

LAMB: Where do you live?

PARINI: In a windy farmhouse in Vermont, built in 1850, not very far from Frost's farm. In the summer I sometimes stay in Frost's house, or I did so for a period, when I was writing this book. In a sense, I've spent my life in Frost country. My first job was teaching at Dartmouth, where Frost had been a student, and I taught there from 1975 through 1982. During my first summer in Hanover, New Hampshire, I went into the rare books and manuscripts room at the Baker Library and encountered the Frost Papers. I began pawing my way through his letters and notebooks, journals and rough drafts. I became fascinated with this man's life and work, started interviewing people who knew Frost, thinking I'd write a biography. And then I moved to Middlebury College, where Frost spent the last decades of his life, in Ripton, which is just outside of Middlebury. He was one of the founders of Middlebury's well-known Bread Loaf Writers' Conference. So through my entire adult life—from the age of twenty-six or so, I've been living in Frost's shadow. As a consequence, I know its feel, the smells, the way the light falls, the background noises.

LAMB: What about the home in Derry, New Hampshire? Is that also set aside as a museum?

PARINI: That's set aside, too, like the house in Ripton. Several of Frost's farmhouses have been restored, turned into tourist destinations. Derry is interesting. Frost, at the age of twenty-five, was a complete failure, had dropped out of Dartmouth, then Harvard. He was a young married man, with several kids and no prospects. So his paternal grandfather set him up with a farmhouse in Derry, New Hampshire, and it was in Derry that a good deal of his finest poetry was written when he was completely unknown. *A Boy's Will* and *North of Boston* go back to that time. Many of the poems we remember were written then. He lived the life of a subsistence farmer and supported his farming with a little bit of teaching at the Pinkerton Academy, then later at a normal school, a school for teachers. At thirty-eight, you know, he still had nothing published. He had four kids, quickly growing, eating a lot of food. He had a wife, Elinor, who was very devoted, but often ill. He was, himself, unwell a lot of the time, prone to lung ailments. In what seems like a rash gesture, he sold the farm and took off for England. That was in 1912–1915—a period when he really put his first two books together, got them published first in England. When Frost arrived on American shores in 1915, he walked up to a newsstand and saw the *New Republic*. He couldn't believe it when he saw his name on the front page—a headline that welcomed a major new poet to the world. Amy Lowell wrote the review. From that point on, Frost was a famous poet, if there *is* such a thing. It's almost a contradiction in terms. But Frost was surely the most celebrated American poet for many decades, at least on this side of the Atlantic.

LAMB: How old was he when he died?

PARINI: Eighty-nine and vigorous to the end. Only a few months before his death in 1963 John Kennedy sent him as a goodwill ambassador to Russia, where he had an incredibly testy head-on conversation with Nikita Khrushchev. It's quite a story. I talk about this in the book, toward the end. F. D. Reeve was a young poet who accompanied him. Reeve was himself a poet, and he knew Russian. He wrote an account of this journey.

LAMB: I want to read you something that you wrote. "He was a Democrat who hated FDR. He was a poet of labor who didn't support the New Deal. He believed in war but was against World War II. He supported Ike and also supported JFK. And he was an anti-Communist who embraced Nikita Khrushchev."
PARINI: A man of contradictions. He reveled in contradiction, having what he called "a lover's quarrel with the world." If any man ever wished to have everything always at once, it was Frost. He wanted to be the poet of the people and a totally independent bard.

LAMB: Whatever was the reason for sending him to Russia?
PARINI: He'd recently attended a conference in Brazil, where he represented the U.S. government as a cultural ambassador. This was the height of the Cold War, and Kennedy understood that they loved poets in Russia. Frost was hugely popular there. The day he arrived in Moscow there was a front-page article in *Pravda*, and they said, "Robert Frost is a true poet of the people. He is a farmer. He's a real working man." In its way, this was true. When you think about it, Frost's greatest poems are about simple people. They're about working. Most of his poems center on activities, such as chopping up wood in "Two Tramps in Mud Time" or "Mowing," a poem about mowing the grass, or "Putting in the Seed," which speaks for itself in the title, or my favorite among all Frost poems—"After Apple-Picking." Frost had done all these things. To the end of his life he kept a farm, even in the last years. He usually had a stand of apple trees and a big garden. He was a part-time farmer much of his adult life. "I like to keep a farm in my back yard," he would say to interviewers.

LAMB: How many places are there that have been set aside like Derry, New Hampshire, and Ripton, Vermont?
PARINI: Well, there's Franconia, in New Hampshire, and another house near Bennington, in South Shaftsbury. So really, four Frost houses are widely known.

LAMB: Have you been to all these places?
PARINI: Yes, and spent a night or more in most of them.

LAMB: What do you get out of doing that?

PARINI: When you go to a poet's house and sit in the chairs, look out the windows, walk the property, I think that you are able to absorb the aura of the writer.

LAMB: Which is your favorite, by the way?

PARINI: The Homer Noble Farm in Ripton, Vermont. The Frost cabin behind the main house is special. I once played a trick on my Middlebury students. I teach a Frost seminar every fall. And recently I was teaching Frost, and I said, "We're going to have this final class in the Frost cabin. It's become a tradition for this seminar." I took the class up there one afternoon, but I'd gone up there the morning before and planted a boom box with a tape of Frost reading behind the sofa. We all sat in the living room and I started talking. I'm able to keep going about Frost for hours, without a pause. I probably talked for two or three hours about Frost's poetry nonstop as the dusk settled. And I purposefully did not turn a light on. Finally, it was pitch-black in the cabin and the students thought, "Jay Parini is going crazy." I let myself run on—seem like I was getting madder and madder, until finally I said, "You know, sometimes at this time of night when you sit here in Frost's cabin, you can almost hear him speaking. I mean, his presence becomes absolutely vivid in the room." Hidden from their view, I pressed the remote in my pocket, and suddenly you heard in a booming voice, "Two roads diverged in a yellow wood / And sorry I could not travel both and be one traveler / Long I stood and looked down one as far as I could." The class nearly panicked. It was wonderful—my best teaching moment in decades.

LAMB: You like "The Road Not Taken."

PARINI: A perfect example of Frost's canny approach to verse writing. It embodies the contradictions in Frost. It seems quite simple on the surface. I think back to my first encounter with Frost in high school. A teacher of mine had framed above her desk the great lines: "I took the road less traveled by / And that has made all the difference." She said to the class, "Let's say those lines together." And the class all repeated, "I took the road less traveled by / And that has made all the difference." With a fierce look in her eye, she told us, "Now I want you to heed that advice. Go your own way. Be your own man. March to the beat of a different drummer." But then I started reading the poem closely. Frost is telling us that these roads are identical. Have you ever noticed that? "And both that morning equally lay / In leaves no step had trodden black." Yet he ends, "I shall be telling this with a sigh, / Somewhere ages and ages hence: / Two roads diverged in a wood, and I— /

I took the one less traveled by, / And that has made all the difference." My God, he's insisted for three stanzas that these roads are identical, "really about the same." So what's going on? Frost wants to say something like this: "I know I'm writing this as a young man in my thirties, and yet I know that as an old man I'm going to sit in my chair, my grandchildren around my feet, and I'm going to lie right through my teeth, telling them that I took the less traveled road." That sigh in the last stanza is a gasp of recognition, a way of acknowledging that the roads were the same all along; that he did not take necessarily the road less traveled. But we all want to think we have taken the road less traveled, at least at the end of our lives. That's a human wish. And Frost was able to pinpoint that irony. He stumbled upon little truths, again and again. It's the miracle of his poetry.

LAMB: Here is a picture of Frost in England, near his house there. Where is that?
PARINI: That house is Little Iddens, a cottage that the Frost family rented in Gloucestershire. That's when he met Edward Thomas, a journalist whom he encouraged to write poems.

LAMB: And what happened to Edward Thomas?
PARINI: Thomas and Frost forged a bond of intense friendship, the most exhilarating friendship with another man that Frost ever had. They reinforced each other. They critiqued each other's poetry, supported each other, discussed what poetry was and what it meant to the world. And Frost was upset when he said goodbye to Thomas in 1915; because of the war, he had to go back to America with his family. It was no longer possible to stay comfortably in Britain. Thomas joined the British Army soon after that, went off as an officer—he was a specialist in reading maps—and was killed at Arras, in France, a devastating blow to Robert Frost. A very bad blow to English poetry as well.

LAMB: Here's a picture of Frost in Franconia. Who is that with him?
PARINI: His son, Carol, who later committed suicide at the farm near Bennington. Frost had a very sad life, you know. So many deaths, so much sickness, a lot of mental illness in the family. His life was quite chaotic. He was fairly depressive through much of his life, either manic or depressed. He oscillated back and forth between poles. His wife, Elinor, was fragile. His daughter, Irma, was hospitalized for emotional problems, and she died in an institution. His beloved daughter, Marjorie, died in childbirth—a huge blow. One child, Elliott, was only four when he died from an infection. In

Frost's family there is one disaster after another. The wonder is that he got through it at all, and with such buoyancy and spirit. Every poem was essentially a triumph over the chaos that surrounded him. Frost regarded his life as a tangled wood. You look at a poem like "Directive," and it's essentially a guide to Frost's work. The poem ends at a stream in the woods, the source of all poetry. It's not unlike the Helicon, the stream that flowed off Parnassus, an inspiration. Frost says, "Here are your waters and your watering place. / Drink and be whole beyond confusion." Frost defined poetry as a momentary stay against confusion. And I would stress two words there, momentary and confusion. Poetry, while you're reading it, or writing it, offers clarification, a point of balance.

LAMB: You say at one point that in about 1958 or so he was responsible for bringing culture and politics together, when he was a consultant at the Library of Congress.
PARINI: Before Frost, poets were invisible on the political landscape. We did not have, in the twentieth century, a national bard, so to speak, until Frost arrived on the scene. And he understood that it was important for someone to represent poetry in the way, say, a Poet Laureate does. Poetry needs an advocate in the public realm. And we need to keep bringing the values of poetry to public consciousness. In my view, Frost was very good at doing that.

LAMB: Where did you grow up?
PARINI: I grew up in Scranton, Pennsylvania. A very un-Frostian landscape. Anthracite country. The woods in Scranton were not "lovely, dark and deep." The junkyards were pretty deep, however.

LAMB: What were your parents doing?
PARINI: My father moved between life insurance and eternal life insurance. He was a businessman. In the middle of his life, he became a devout Christian, was ordained, and moved back and forth between the church and the office. It was a Baptist church. My own appreciation for language and poetry started there, at the breakfast table in Scranton. Every morning my father would read to me and my sister, Dorrie, from the Bible, often from the Old Testament. So the rhythms of the Old Testament, the rhythms of scriptural writing, became part of my syntax and diction. I became wedded to those rhythms and that language. I discovered the power of poetry by reading the King James Version of the Bible in my early years.

LAMB: What about your mom?

PARINI: She came from an English background, but was not herself literary. She was a great reader, however.

LAMB: Are they alive?

PARINI: Yes, and still living in Scranton. They're in their early eighties, and I see them regularly. I go back to Scranton often. My first books were centered on Scranton. I wrote an early novel called *The Patch Boys*—an evocation of northeastern Pennsylvania during the twenties, my father's era. *Huck Finn* on the Susquehanna, that's how I think of that book. And my first real book of poems was called *Anthracite Country*, published in 1982. These were mostly poems about growing up in coal country, vignettes from childhood. I was trying to find my own language, trying to describe and picture my childhood in rhythms, with images that seemed adequate to my experience. My early poems were highly visual, often narrative, easy to read, at least I like to think so. I played with conventional forms: sonnets, even villanelles, heroic couplets, blank verse. But you can hear the poets I fed on: Hopkins, Frost and Heaney, Eliot, Theodore Roethke. I wrote my master's thesis on Hopkins at St. Andrews, in Scotland. My master's thesis was a study of the influence of Ignatius Loyola on Gerard Manley Hopkins. I did a doctoral dissertation on Roethke and the traditions of American Romanticism. I've always been very wedded to the ideas of Emerson, and that plays through my Roethke book. I have turned to Emerson, as a thinker, repeatedly throughout my life. He is, as I think Matthew Arnold said, the "aid and abettor of all who would live in the spirit." I grow more fond of him by the decade.

LAMB: I counted thirteen books: five novels, four books of poetry, one textbook, one book of essays on writing and politics, a biography of John Steinbeck.

PARINI: Too many books for anyone to write.

LAMB: What's the book on politics and writing?

PARINI: It's a collection of essays that I've written over the last twenty years. The first section is divided into personal essays, including an essay on mentors, another on playing baseball as a young teen. In that section of personal essays are several essays on politics where I play off Thomas Mann's *Confessions of a Non-Political Man.* I had been deeply political in the late sixties, protesting the Vietnam War. I retreated from that a bit, when the war ended; but in the mid-eighties I realized that I couldn't avoid politics, that it was impossible. A writer has to say what he or she sees. I've spoken bluntly about things, and that, I think, becomes a political act. People who know how to use language, who read deeply, who are reflective and who care about their society, they shouldn't stick their head in the sand. There is so much false language around us, in the press, everywhere. Poets look for real words that attach to real feelings. This is inherently a political act. We need poetry and good prose because we need voices to remind us of realities we won't get from listening to politicians talk or reading newspapers or magazines or listening to pundits on television. The work of knowing, that's what poets and other "real" writers do. They discover the truth, as they see it, and they embody those truths in language.

LAMB: Before we go on to anything else, I want to ask you about Wallace Stevens, another Pennsylvanian. He and Robert Frost had a relationship. Who was he, and how did he come up in your books?
PARINI: In some ways, the three great American poets of the twentieth century are T. S. Eliot, Robert Frost, and Wallace Stevens. And they could not be more different. Stevens—we've talked about T. S. Eliot and his relationship to Frost, which was troubled. The relationship with Wallace Stevens was just as difficult. Stevens was an insurance man who worked for the Accident and Indemnity Company in Hartford, and he became a vice president of that company. He put on his banker's suit and lived in the suburbs—and every day walked down an elm-lined street to his office. He would go home at night, climb the stairs to his attic, lock his door and take out his Cuban cigars and open a bottle of fine French wine and write poetry. He wrote a sensuous, philosophical poetry that could not be more different from the poetry of Frost. These poets could not understand each other. In fact, Frost ran into Wallace Stevens once in Key West, and they had a little exchange. Frost said to Stevens, "Your poetry is too full of bric-a-brac." That is, it's full of fancy French words, made-up words, neologisms. It's elaborately shaped, with curlicues of language and thought. Stevens follows in the tradition of the French aesthetes, art for art's sake, whereas Robert Frost was writing about the working man, plainspoken things, but in beautiful language.

LAMB: There's another story I wanted you to tell about the fire and Archibald MacLeish.
PARINI: Frost was often jealous of other poets. MacLeish was giving a poetry reading at the Bread Loaf Writers' Conference in what we call the little

theater one night, in 1938, and Frost was sitting in the front row. As Ma-cLeish read, Frost took up his *New York Times* and, page by page, began to crumple it up. He built a mound of these pages on the seat beside him, then took out a match, lit it and—whoosh—a bonfire flared. And he yelled, "Fire! Fire!" The audience panicked and fled from the building. Of course Frost was persona non grata at the conference for the rest of that summer. MacLeish said, "Robert, you're a good poet, but you're a very bad man." That may partly be true. But what I do in my biography is take all of these nasty stories about Frost, and put them in the context of Frost's difficult personal life. This was 1938, August of 1938. In June of 1938, Frost's beloved wife of more than three decades, Elinor, died of a heart attack. He was devastated. I came across the journals of a young poet, Charles Foster, who had dinner with Frost most nights at Bread Loaf. I quote the journals where he said, more or less, "Frost was wild with grief." Frost told him he was crazy with grief. He couldn't seem to hold his life together. It was a dark time.

LAMB: Didn't he have an affair with Kay Morrison before his wife died?
PARINI: He might have loved her and was attracted to her. But I believe he was faithful to Elinor while she was alive. The romance with Kay subsided into kind of a Platonic relationship within a fairly short time. That's my intuition. One never knows.

LAMB: Could you clarify the feelings Frost had about teaching, about college?
PARINI: We're back to paradox, in that Frost wanted everything both ways. He was himself an inconsistent student in college, did not like the discipline of the classroom and did not like orderly knowledge. He was lazy by nature. Neither Dartmouth nor Harvard appealed to him. He was not disciplined, even as a reader. He and school didn't get along, although he liked teaching, at least part-time.

LAMB: How much teaching did he do?
PARINI: From 1917, when he was invited to join the faculty at Amherst, he taught in a part-time fashion. He kept a lifelong connection with Amherst, and it was the only college where he taught seriously. He had some periods at the University of Michigan. There was a little stretch when he taught at Dartmouth as the Ticknor Fellow. And there was a brief while as visiting lecturer at Harvard. Then, as I said, in the summers he would teach and read at the Bread Loaf Writers' Conference, which is part of Middlebury Col-

lege. He founded the conference there, in 1927. But for the most part, Frost believed that the function of the writer in the academy was to be a presence, to show a contrasting way of knowledge. In his beautiful essay "The Figure a Poem Makes," he writes about the different approaches to learning, to knowledge. And he says that the scholar makes a systematized effort. The poet skips forward and backward, this way and that way, darts to and fro, stumbles upon insights. It's accidental knowledge. That's the paradoxical nature of Frost again. And as a teacher, he was disorganized. A few students couldn't stand it. There was no set program, little in the way of a syllabus. Frost taught himself. Yet his conversation was riveting. You wanted to sit in the room and listen. Of course Frost believed deeply in poetry, especially in the function—even the usefulness—of metaphor. He says, in an essay called "Education by Poetry," that unless you're educated in metaphor and have a grounding in how metaphor works, you're not safe to be let loose in the world.

LAMB: What was the story about Stark Young at Amherst?
PARINI: That's a sad story, I think. Frost was a man of fierce prejudices. This isn't surprising for the period, but I would say that in today's term he would be considered anti-gay. He sensed that Young, this aesthetic young professor, who wrote novels and plays and lots of critical essays, was gay. Young was one of the most popular teachers at Amherst College at the time—he taught there from 1915 through 1921. Frost joined forces with those who disliked Young, and he did everything he could to get him fired. He didn't succeed, but he tried hard. And Frost even took against the very people who supported him, including Alexander Meiklejohn, a philosopher, the president of Amherst who actually hired Frost. Frost was sitting on his porch in Franconia. He was a lazy farmer. This was in the hot summer of 1917. Meiklejohn appeared with Young, as they both admired Frost's poetry. Meiklejohn said, "Look, why don't you come down and try your hand as a visiting writer at Amherst College? Just one term, give it a shot." Frost agreed, and a lifelong connection to that college was established.

LAMB: How did he do there?
PARINI: He loved the contact with students, liked—for the most part—having colleagues. He enjoyed being able to put forward his opinions on things, to test these opinions on the air. As I've discovered, having taught throughout my adult life, one of the great things about living in an academic community is that whatever you say will get shot down and turned around.

You're always testing your thoughts against others. Academic life is a contest: the word "campus" comes from a Latin word meaning contest. It's a contest of ideas. And Frost loved the to and fro of the academic village. He was very playful. He liked the back and forth of intellectual combat. But he could be mean at times, and he became rather vicious about Stark Young. He sided with a group of faculty who opposed Young. Nothing was said about Young's homosexuality. It was all innuendo in those days.

LAMB: Going back to Lawrence Thompson, who we started out talking about. You say that Thompson suggested that Frost was a selfish, egomaniacal, cruel, and an angry man. Do you disagree with any of that?
PARINI: No. Frost was all of those things. He was angry and jealous. I think he was mean-spirited, at times. On the other hand, he was generous to many people, and he was kind to his students. He was devoted to his family and his wife, even though he could be horrible to them as well. As ever, he was a man of contradictory impulses.

LAMB: Thompson called him a monster.
PARINI: Repeatedly. And that's where I draw the line. Frost was a difficult man but a great artist who lived in trying personal circumstances. I don't whitewash Frost: he could be jealous and temperamental, selfish and willful. But he was hardly a monster. That's a foolish exaggeration of the facts, and it doesn't take into account the complexity of the situation.

LAMB: Twenty years you spent with Robert Frost, in getting this book out. When you left Scranton, where'd you go to school?
PARINI: To Lafayette College in Easton, Pennsylvania—a really beautiful campus, and I had good teachers. I took my junior year abroad at the University of St. Andrews in Scotland—another beautiful spot. It's on the North Sea, a haunting place. I loved it there. Students wore scarlet gowns, spent a lot of time in pubs. I liked it so I returned briefly to finish my degree at Lafayette, then scooted back to Scotland for another five years and did a couple of degrees. I began writing poetry seriously during my junior year in St. Andrews, although I'd been writing a little from my teenage years onward. I was lucky that a poet called Alastair Reid became my mentor and friend in Scotland. I would pedal on my bicycle every day out to Alastair's cottage on the Old Course—the first golf course in the world, in fact. I would arrive with a damp poem and put it on Alastair's kitchen table. We would sip a cup of tea while he would cross out and add lines. He'd say, "I'll correct

your poem." It was an allusion to his own life. He went to Mallorca to work as a secretary to Robert Graves. Graves asked Alastair to sit beside him, and he "corrected" Alastair's work, making it tighter and stronger. Adjectives would disappear, absorbed into stronger nouns. Adverbs were crossed out, and stronger verbs inserted. I published my first book of poems when I was a graduate student there—*Singing in Time*. It was juvenilia, but it got me going. I met a number of poets during my years in Scotland, including Anne Stevenson, another close friend. I went up to the Orkney Islands to visit George Mackay Brown, a poet and novelist, a writer of haunting stories. I met, briefly, Auden and Spender. It was all very exciting for a kid from Scranton.

LAMB: Where have you been located in schools so far?
PARINI: Dartmouth and Middlebury College—both in New England. With a year at Christ Church, Oxford, as a visiting fellow.

LAMB: And family?
PARINI: I have a wonderful wife of many years, whom I met at Dartmouth. We have three boys.

LAMB: Any of them poets?
PARINI: The two older boys are teenagers, and they're more interested in skateboarding and snowboarding. My oldest boy is a terrific guitar player, and he writes his own songs. My middle son is very philosophical, naturally wise, well-balanced and quick. The young one is still a kid, although he's bright and funny. You can see that right away when you meet him.

LAMB: By the way, where'd you write this book?
PARINI: On the backs of envelopes, traveling here and there, in my study, in cafes. I'm not fussy about where I write. I don't worry about noise or light or anything like that. I wrote my first novel by hand, in a freezing room in Scotland, wearing gloves in a vast, empty room in Parliament Hall in St. Andrews—a room where the Scottish parliament met briefly hundreds of years ago. I still write by hand—all my poems are first hand-written. I type things up afterward, on my computer.

LAMB: What's next?
PARINI: Let me see, it's been a busy time for me and I've had four books out in the last two years: the book of essays; the novel called *Benjamin's*

Crossing, about the life of Walter Benjamin, a German-Jewish intellectual who was chased by the Nazis over the Pyrenees into Spain; a book of poems, *House of Days*, was published last year by Henry Holt, Frost's publisher; and now the Frost biography. I'm writing poems, and I'm working on a novel. Who isn't? I don't know what I'll do, whether I'll write another biography or not. I don't worry about these things. Must see what comes. I'll always be writing poems. That's all I count on.

An Interview with Jay Parini

Paul Holler / 2006

From *Bookslut* with Paul Holler (April 2006): http://www.bookslut.com/fea
tures/2006_04_008406.php. Reprinted by permission.

The works of Jay Parini have crossed many literary boundaries and blurred
many more. His novels have told of both his own experiences growing up
in the coal mining region of Pennsylvania and that of literary icons facing
their own ends. His nonfiction works include biographies of John Steinbeck,
Robert Frost, and William Faulkner. His poetry, essays, and criticism reflect
both the events of his own life and his political views. For the past thirty
years, Mr. Parini has taught undergraduate courses at Middlebury College
in Vermont.

I recently spoke with Mr. Parini about his work, the world it reflects.

"I write because I like doing it," says Mr. Parini. "I can't wait to get out
my notebook in the morning and to start. I usually begin the day by working on poetry. I love that moment, when I first open the blank page, and
when I begin to hear the voice accumulating in my head, then transferring
that energy to the page. I write poems in longhand, in a notebook; later, I
type them into a computer. But I do many revisions by hand first, in my
notebook. I like the feel of writing fiction and criticism, too; I work on these
after I've finished with the poetry for the day. Novels are absorbing projects.
I submerse myself in the subject, when I'm working on a novel; it's always
there, somewhere, on my mind. Criticism and biography have their own
charms, too, and I like to do them as a break from the strictly creative work,
although I don't really see much difference between a novel and a biography;
in both cases, you're selecting among a zillion possible facts, finding a narrative, creating order from chaos. It's what the poet Wallace Stevens called
that "blessed rage for order" in "The Idea of Order at Key West." I like to
use language, and it's thrilling to let the language roll off the fingers, off the
mental tongue. I feel grounded when I'm writing, which is probably the real

reason I write. When I don't write, I feel disconnected from the world, and that is an uncomfortable feeling.

"I began as a poet, in high school. I wrote poems through college, with considerable focus after the beginning of my junior year, in Scotland. I read and wrote poetry avidly as a young man. I came to fiction a bit later, writing a novel in graduate school, when I was perhaps twenty-three or twenty-four. It was never published, and it was not good. I wrote part of another novel, and it, too, lacked sufficient energy, lacked narrative momentum. I never tried to publish my early fiction. But I took up novel writing again at around the age of thirty, writing *The Love Run* more for my own amusement. It was a rotten book, I admit. I think my frustration with the failure of that book got me writing *The Patch Boys*, which took five or six years. I remember rewriting the whole novel, taking it from third person to first. I had many different endings. It was exhausting work.

"Yet I never stopped writing poetry. I've always written poetry as a primary occupation, adding fiction and criticism as other ways of using language. *The Last Station*, a novel about the last year of Tolstoy's life, was my first mature novel, and I loved writing it. Same with the other novels, such as *Benjamin's Crossing* or *The Apprentice Lover*. I loved writing those books. It amazes me to see I've published six novels, with a seventh on the way. I never thought of myself as a novelist. But I have ideas for half a dozen more novels, so I guess I'm a novelist. In the past few years, however, I've returned to the poetry with considerable energy, writing a new kind of political poem in response to the invasions of Iraq and Afghanistan. I think poetry often comes from fury, and it did in the wake of George W. Bush, the most disastrous American president in history. I feel quite excited about my *New and Selected Poems*—it has a long section of new work, with some of my better work there, such as the villanelle called "After the Terror," a response to 9/11. I still write reviews and essays, as the situations arise for these. I'm more or less finished with biography, having just published a life of William Faulkner.

"I make few distinctions between straight biographies and novels. They are works of fiction. The story of a life can be told in the conventional way of biography, which I find less satisfactory, or in fictional form. Fiction allows you more freedom: you can imagine motives, dig into the unconscious of a character, get inside a character's head. A biographer would write: 'Sofya Tolstoy threw herself into a pond in the summer of 1910, upset about her husband's disappearance.' A novelist can go inside her emotions, imagine what it really felt like to be in her pressured situation."

The decision to write about a famous literary figure can speak to the author's personal taste and the tastes of the reading public. But the decision of whether to cast that book as a work of fiction or as straight biography speaks to both the craft of the writer and the nature of the subject. I asked Mr. Parini about *Benjamin's Crossing*, his novel of Walter Benjamin, the German-Jewish intellectual chased by the Nazis over the Pyrenees in 1940. Not unlike *The Last Station*, it unfolds from different viewpoints.

"I see Benjamin as an archetype of the Old World intellectual, a man who knew the classics, who read widely in literature and philosophy and politics, who knew the history of the world," says Mr. Parini. "He was not a specialist, and this attracted me to him as well. He wrote stories, and his essays ranged widely from the personal to the theoretical. He debated the major issues of his time. He was part of the larger conversation of the world of thinkers.

"This all caught my attention, plus the fact that he was caught in a very bad time and had to flee from the Nazis. The story struck me as a natural novel for me, one rooted in facts. I did a good deal of research, spent a lot of time with Benjamin and his work. Of course the man you imagine is always at some distance from the actual man; I accept that. The Benjamin of my novel is a work of fiction, a made-up character, but a character with some allegiance to the historical figure. For example, I keep the dates and places the same. The basic outline of his life and his ideas are accurate. But I dig into his mind in ways that a straight biographer could never dare to attempt. Conventional biography is fairly rigid, and the biographer can't dig into the subjective consciousness of a subject in the way novelists do.

"With Tolstoy, I loved the work first, then the man. I was attracted to his ideas and to his narratives. I loved his letters and diaries. These led me back to the man and the situation of his life, which seemed especially compelling, especially during that fateful last year when he was so conflicted about where his last days should take him and how he should get there. I loved the drama of that household and the set-pieces that the novel allowed me to write. I think of myself as essentially a Tolstoyan in my spiritual and political life. I often reread Tolstoy, his novels and—in particular—his great essays. *The Kingdom of God Is Within You* is something I could recommend to anyone.

"I've done the three conventional biographies, John Steinbeck, Robert Frost and now Faulkner, which I think will be my last biography of that kind," says Mr. Parini. "These are just three figures who have meant a lot to me over the years. For a long time I'd hoped to write about Faulkner. One of my mentors, a close friend, was Robert Penn Warren. He and I would go for long hikes in the woods in Vermont from the late seventies through the whole decade of the eighties. He urged me to write about Faulkner. I spent one weekend with Warren and Cleanth Brooks and their excited talk about Faulkner sent me back to his novels and stories. I started reading him closely and teaching him regularly. That book is a side product of my personal reading and writing. It offered a way to clarify my own thoughts on Faulkner.

"What I can bring to a biography is a writer's sense of the discipline and commitment it takes to assemble a shelf of books over a lifetime. There's an inherent drama there, the whole cycle of production and rejection, agony, elation, all of the different things that go into producing a body of work. I love tracking that progress (or regress) in a biography, seeing how another writer does it."

It's clear enough why a novelist would be attracted to other literary figures as subjects for biography. But a writer's own life, and the times in which he or she lives, can be the most important of all stories. Flashes of his own life and views occur in many of Mr. Parini's works, but perhaps they appear most frequently in his poetry.

"It's fairly true that I keep poetry—or have kept it—for the most autobiographical and personal stuff," says Mr. Parini about his work in this genre. "My first real book of poems was *Anthracite Country* (1982), and it focused on my childhood in the coal mining region of northeastern Pennsylvania. My grandfather and uncles were miners. One uncle died in the mines—on the day I graduated from high school in 1966. I grew up with the imagery of mining around me, as part of the landscape of my life; this landscape still lives at the back of my mind. I did one Pennsylvania novel, *The Patch Boys*, published in 1986. It's my father's life in fiction, the story of a young man of Italian immigrant parents growing up in the mining country near Scranton. I turned very briefly to that material in *The Apprentice Lover* (2002). The hero of that novel goes to live in Italy as secretary to an older writer, and he's a fellow from near Scranton. The main character—Alex—is an alter-ego of mine, a version of myself, having much the same background. To some extent, it's based on my friend Alastair Reid and his apprenticeship with Robert Graves in Mallorca, though I set the book on the island of Capri, as it was familiar. I've spent a good deal of time on the Amalfi Coast, and I know Capri rather well."

The question of the personal and the political in a writer's work can lead in turn to the question of a writer's responsibility to comment on social issues. Should a writer be a detached observer reporting on events and people? Or should he or she become involved in the political process?

"I see two strands to that question and I'll separate them. The one strand concerns the degree to which any of my political interests turn up in my fiction. I'd have to say that it bears on the fiction rather indirectly. Because the Tolstoy book, *Benjamin's Crossing*, and *The Apprentice Lover* and I suppose even *The Patch Boys*, my early novel, all deal with the question of morality. I deal with the responsibility of the artist to the public events of his day—especially in the later novels. In *The Apprentice Lover*, I wrestle with the memory of Vietnam. That war deeply affected most people of my generation. Obviously, Walter Benjamin's story is about his catastrophic failure to comprehend the severity of the political situation at the moment—as the Second World War began. For all of his intellectual weight and breadth and depth, there was still a sense in which he was naive about the Nazi war machine and the trouble he was in. He stayed in Paris way too late.

"Nevertheless, he was an acutely sensitive political thinker. He was a Marxist. In writing that novel, I held a mirror up to contemporary life and saw this odd reflection, deep in the past. Historical novels often do that. That's probably so with *The Apprentice Lover*, too. As I said, there's a lot in that book about Vietnam. In so many ways Vietnam was the touchstone event in my life. And I've gone back to it mentally over and over again. My poems have crept toward politics for some time. In *Town Life*, there's a poem about Cambodia. I visited the Cambodian refugee camps in the early eighties and wrote about them. So politics gets into the poems as it gets into my life, into everyone's life. And, of course, in the eighties I reawakened to politics with Ronald Reagan and his dreadful interference in Central America. His support for the Contras and for the death squads in El Salvador, his support for right wing elements of Honduras and Guatemala. Those things obsessed me at the time. I had difficulty writing about them and figuring out how to get involved—as a writer. So my political work consisted mostly of letters to the editor and things like that. I spoke up as I could, whenever I could.

"The first time in a really major way I've been able to bring politics into my poetry was *The Art of Subtraction: New and Selected Poems*. The first fifty-four poems in there were new work that dealt explicitly with Bush and the Middle East, with the war on terror. I've tried to write imaginative work that's politically engaged without publishing overt political tracts. I learned something from my friend Adrienne Rich there. She did that sort of thing so well, as in 'What Kind of Times Are These,' an astounding poem that succeeds on every level.

"I did whatever I could think to do during the Iraq War to raise a voice of protest. I was among the group of poets invited to the White House by Bar-

bara Bush, and she canceled the event when the poets spoke out. I worked with a number of friends in a movement called Poets against the War. My good friend and neighbor, Julia Alvarez, joined me on several public occasions to protest the war in public ways. We had a vivid reading in Manchester, Vermont, and were joined by Galway Kinnell, Greg Delanty, Grace Paley, and others. It was a very moving event. I went to the Middle East five or six times to give talks—to engage in dialogue with Islamic students and writers, to get a feel for what was happening. I visited Egypt, Jordan, Israel, the West Bank, and Morocco. These travels brought me into close touch with any number of poets, novelists, and journalists from that region, and I remain in touch with some of them. The dialogue continues. I'm planning to go back to Egypt very soon."

Writer's Craft: Floating Ideas
with Literary Legend Jay Parini

Mike Ives / 2007

From Mike Ives/ *Seven Days* (August 15, 2007): http://www.7dvt.com/2007/writers-craft.
Reprinted by permission.

Jay Parini may be one of this country's most distinguished men of letters. But his summer study is missing a few basic implements. Like, um, a printer. And a front door.

During the academic year, Parini usually starts the day writing poetry in Carol's Hungry Mind Café on Merchant's Row in Middlebury. From there, he heads to class or his campus office for the afternoon. But during June, July, and August, he likes to read, write, and chill aboard his twenty-five-foot motorboat, *Fishin Impossible*.

Although his approach to literary production may seem oddly informal, there's nothing casual about Parini's career: Since the early 1970s, when he began publishing in Scottish newspapers, Parini, fifty-nine, has been banging out poems, essays, novels, biographies, and articles on topics ranging from small-town baseball to early-twentieth-century German intellectuals. Although he travels around the world giving readings and lectures, for twenty-five years Parini has always returned to the environs of Middlebury College, where he's an English professor-cum-amateur-b-baller.

Eight years ago, around the time he traded his old boat for this one, he published a biography of Robert Frost that went on to win the *Chicago Tribune* Heartland Award for best nonfiction book. These days, he still scores book and article contracts as if they were lay-ups on a kids' basket.

How does the writer pull it off? On a recent Wednesday afternoon, I climb aboard *Fishin Impossible* to find out. The journey on Lake Champlain offers a rare glimpse into the creative process of one of Vermont's most celebrated, albeit unassuming, cultural icons.

51

Fishin Impossible lives on Otter Creek at Tom's Marine Service in Vergennes. When I meet Parini there, he's dressed in a pale yellow T-shirt and green khaki shorts. The professor's grin stretches from ear to ear; his face is lathered generously with suntan lotion, so that some of the gunk has settled behind his ears. If it weren't for a shiny bald spot and a pair of thick glasses, he could be an oversized kid looking for frogs. "The best thing about Lake Champlain is that there's hardly anyone on it," he says cheerfully, without drawing attention to the fact that it's a weekday. "That's OK with me!"

In high-summer style, Parini starts up the motor, then bids me pour out two glasses of iced tea. For twenty minutes, we putter down the creek—"like in Heart of Darkness," he suggests. While he steers, I look around his cabin. On the small plastic table next to the iced tea sits a book of Robert Frost's poetry and a thin spiral notebook. Keeping one eye on the horizon, Parini explains that he's co-writing a screenplay about the poet's life.

That's just the tip of his literary iceberg. Turns out the professor has a hand in a slew of other projects. For instance, he's working on a play, *Mary Postgate*—based on a Rudyard Kipling short story—and a nonfiction book entitled *Promised Land: Thirteen Books That Shaped America* (forthcoming from Doubleday). Another nonfiction effort, *Why Poetry Matters*, comes out next year from Yale University Press. A film adaptation of Parini's novel *The Last Station*, which chronicles the last year of Tolstoy's life, begins shooting next year in Russia. That flick will star—ahem—Helen Mirren and Christopher Plummer. Oh, and he has two other novels "in the vault." One of them, called *Anderson Depot*, is set during the American Civil War.

With the sun out in full force, we hit the open lake with our bow aimed straight for the Adirondacks. Parini steps on the accelerator, and the iced-tea pitcher goes flying, soaking the book and the notebook with Marx Brothers slapstick flair. I scramble on my hands and knees, observing, "I ruined your movie, Jay!"

"Don't worry about that!" he shouts over the motor. "Just get a towel, will you!"

I wipe down the books, stow them in the cabin, then return to the cockpit. At thirty miles per hour, the wind alleviates the heat. True to Parini's claim, there are only a handful of other vessels out here today, most of them sailboats. As we begin heading north toward Kingsland Bay State Park, the writer points out notable landmarks. Straight ahead is Point Bay Marina. On a bluff to our right looms a craggy mansion. "Look at that," Parini notes, raising his eyebrows. "It's like something out of *Wuthering Heights*"—Emily Brontë's dark novel set in mid-nineteenth-century northern England.

Parini doesn't live in a spooky English castle, but he does exude a palpable literary mystique. Though born in gritty Scranton, Pennsylvania, he's spent many years of his adult life living in the U.K. and Italy, all the while rubbing shoulders with some of the world's most renowned authors. Back in the early seventies, for instance, he studied with the Scottish poet and essayist Alastair Reid while completing graduate work at the University of St. Andrews. His neighbor in Italy was the American writer and social critic Gore Vidal.

Now, having established himself as a prominent wordsmith, Parini appears to get more speaking offers than a presidential candidate. The author, who still writes on literary topics for the London-based newspaper the *Guardian*, recently toured Belarus, Jordan, Egypt, Palestine, and Israel as a U.S. State Department–sponsored lecturer on American literature and writing. Next year, the government has arranged for him to talk in Morocco. "I've always been a little peripatetic since I was nineteen," he says modestly as we catch a mooring in Kingsland Bay.

In spite of his internationalism, however, Parini remains . . . well, a guy who grew up in Scranton. Once we've caught a mooring in Kingsland Bay, he changes into a pair of goofy red swim trunks emblazoned with little anchors. We dive into the lake and float around for forty minutes, neither of us attempting much more than pseudo-doggie paddle. "When I'm swimming, I feel like I'm part fish!" he jokes at one point.

That may sound silly coming from a guy who has been on the fiction jury for the National Book Award. But for this writer, kicking back isn't merely a distraction from the real world. Handing me a microbrew back on the boat, Parini explains that "creative leisure" is a vital ingredient in his creative stew. Just like a café, this boat offers time and space for inspiration to bubble up. "Frost once said that he was very lazy, and that it was the only way he could get anything done," Parini explains. "I could never get anything done if I didn't have an immense amount of free time."

That doesn't mean all his days are "productive" in the conventional sense. As we sip our drinks on this sunny afternoon, Parini pauses to ogle a polished wooden motorboat that's moving across the harbor. Gazing at the antique craft, he confides that sometimes he'll spend hours reading boating magazines here in Kingsland Bay. "There are whole days when I just sit here," he says. "I've never made a big distinction between work and play. If I wasn't enjoying a class or a novel I'm writing, I'd do a terrible job of it."

At first glance, Parini's worldly and small-town sensibilities might seem diametrically opposed. Not so. In spite of a busy travel schedule, he makes a point of staying connected to this region. Why Vermont, of all places? Parini has always enjoyed what he terms "town life." And he says this state feels most comfortable to him precisely because it's the least American of them all. "For the most part, I'm turned off by the commercialization of America and the right-wing politics," he admits. "I can't even read the papers . . . Even the *New York Times* gives me a lot of trouble."

Though Parini might be tempted to tune out entirely, in the tradition of so many other disillusioned American writers—e.g., fellow boating enthusiast Ernest Hemingway—he says he never will. A vocal opponent of the Iraq war, he feels "a duty to contribute to the [public] discourse in any way I can." That explains why he periodically takes breaks from his various literary projects to contribute to the *Chronicle of Higher Education*, *Vermont Life*, and Vermont Public Radio. "I'm always complaining about American intellectual life," Parini adds, "so I'd feel like a hypocrite if I didn't have an oar in the water."

Fortunately for this thinker, literature—like his boat—offers an easy escape from world events. As the sun starts to drop behind the Adirondacks, Parini gushes about the power of the written word, but in a tone that's still conversational and unpretentious. He recalls escaping from Scranton through the prose of Robert Louis Stevenson and Sir Walter Scott. Here on the boat, he'll pick up Walt Whitman and be similarly transported to other landscapes and mental climes.

Meanwhile, it's about time to head home. Just before he asks me to retrieve our bowline, he gestures at a nearby outcropping of rocks where a woman in a bathing suit has been reading a book. "It's the universal library— a phrase of Borges's," he reflects. "We carry [literature] in our head. Reading allows us to travel constantly."

Parini smiles, then finishes his thought. "The experience of swimming and then lying on a rock on the shore," he points out, "hasn't changed for over ten centuries."

Jay Parini's *The Last Station*: Tolstoy's Final Year

Ramona Koval / 2007

From Radio National's *The Book Show* (October 11, 2007): http://www.abc.net.au/radio national/programs/bookshow/jay-parinis-last-station-tolstoys-final-year/3219250. Repro-duced by permission of the Australian Broadcasting Corporation and ABC online. © 2007 ABC.

Ramona Koval: Jay Parini's *The Last Station* was published to great acclaim in 1990. It concerned the final year in the life of the great Russian writer as he was surrounded by some of his family, some of his acolytes, his secretary, and others. While his wife Sofya was concerned that he leave his estate to her and the children, he is torn between her demands, his duty as a husband and father, his obligations to his followers, and his philosophical and religious beliefs. The book is about to be rereleased to coincide with a film starring Christopher Plummer as Tolstoy and Helen Mirren as Mrs. Tolstoy.

Jay Parini is a poet, a professor of English at Middlebury College in Vermont, a critic as well as a novelist. His nonfiction works include biographies of John Steinbeck, Robert Frost, and William Faulkner. He was the editor of the *Oxford Encyclopedia of American Literature* in 2004. And Parini joins us from his home in Vermont in the U.S.A. Welcome to *The Book Show*, Jay.

Jay Parini: Thank you, Ramona, it's fun to be on the radio here in Australia, at least by phone.

Ramona Koval: It was quite a year, that last one, for the eighty-two-year-old Tolstoy. It was 1910, and it's not giving away too much to say that this old man ran away from home in despair.

Jay Parini: Everything converged on him in one fell swoop. Here's a man who had devoted himself to writing and then he became a religious convert, a devout Christian, although he forged his own theology. He preached chastity and poverty. He thought that one should give all one's earthly possessions to God, to the people. Yet there he was living on this great estate, he was a nobleman, with thousands of former serfs still on the property, under his supervision, depending on him for their living. He had thirteen children, a rather aggressive and difficult and quite wonderful wife, and he could not easily control his sexual impulses. The contradictions in his life overwhelmed him, as they would.

Ramona Koval: And it's all very well for him to preach chastity, but he had rather an unchaste life up until then.

Jay Parini: He was a lusty fellow by nature. It's not surprising that Anthony Quinn wanted to play him. He and I wrote many versions of a script for this film, although Tony died before the film could be made. Quinn was taken by Tolstoy's wandering eye. If you read Tolstoy's diaries, he would put stars in places where he failed to live up to the level of chastity that he preached.

Ramona Koval: So it was star-covered?

Jay Parini: A Milky Way of infidelity. He would sometimes write "failed once again." His failures plagued him.

Ramona Koval: Try again, fail again, fail better. Would it be true to say that almost no other great twentieth-century writer had a life that was so extensively documented as Tolstoy's?

Jay Parini: It's hard to think of anyone. Tolstoy never woke up in the morning that there wasn't a gang of reporters sitting outside waiting for him. They were photographing him. The last scene in my novel, Tolstoy's death in the railway station, was chronicled by one of the first Pathé news camera teams. A small tent city of reporters camped near the little house where he was dying. Before that, much of Tolstoy's life was recorded by Tolstoy in his voluminous diaries. As you know, I based this book on the various diaries that were written by family and friends around Tolstoy.

Ramona Koval: How did you begin to use these texts?

Jay Parini: Frequently the diaries overlapped, and so I got a real sense of how Tolstoy actually talked, as they recorded him speaking to his servants, to friends, his wife and children. Of course *The Last Station* is a novel, a work of imagination. I felt I was able to work my way imaginatively into Tolstoy's world with the help of these texts. In the narrative I speak from multiple points of view, six or seven angles, creating voices. Anytime Tolstoy speaks, though, I report something he said or quote from his actual writings. I didn't dare write in the voice of Leo Tolstoy. That would have been hubris.

Ramona Koval: You used some of his letters, too?

Jay Parini: Yes, lots of his letters, and they're real letters. He had a gift for correspondence. The novel is factually accurate, I should point out. I was lucky to have my old friend from St. Andrews, in Scotland—a major Russian scholar called Reginald Christian—go through the novel in manuscript. He saved me from myself on many occasions, brought the book back to historical and literary realities. I've always made sure to draw on expert advice when writing a biographical novel or a biography.

Ramona Koval: Let's talk about the relationship between Sofya and Tolstoy.

Jay Parini: She helped him rewrite *War and Peace*, copying it many times. Six times! She was at his side at every moment, his secretary and best friend, a critic and reader and lover, mother of his children and manager of his finances. She pretty much ran this large estate. He could devote himself to reading and thinking, to writing. He was hugely prolific.

Ramona Koval: So how do you see the development of their relationship to that last year, where she is off her head, furious with him, attempting suicide all the time. They have an angry relationship, and he seems like an old man hounded by this woman.

Jay Parini: He was something of a fanatic, pushing everything to the extreme. I'm sympathetic with Sofya on that front. It's difficult to live with such a person. Yet he had a deep spiritual core, and he felt the contradictions in his life and realized that in fact the material things are ephemeral, they pass away. He believed that one should live ultimately for spiritual values. As he grew older he became more conscious of the contradictions in his life and, as a consequence, became less tolerant of his wife. At the end, he couldn't stand it any longer, and he just wanted to break free, to give up all worldly goods. Of course his wife would have none of this.

Ramona Koval: And she's really canny about his copyright, isn't she, and she doesn't want him to change his will. She only really has access to his copyright up to a certain time.

Jay Parini: Sure, she thought she should have all the copyright. The money was in *War and Peace* and *Anna Karenina* and all the great works. The religious and philosophical works had less of an audience, less commercial value. It's hard to imagine how famous Tolstoy was in his day. Tolstoy was immensely popular worldwide. Sofya knew it was expensive to keep up a big estate, to sustain a family of that size. She wanted the money.

Ramona Koval: Let's talk about her for a moment because I just saw a new book that's been discussed in the *Literary Review* coming out of London, *Song without Words: The Photographs and Diaries of Countess Sofya Tolstoy* by Leah Bendavid-Val, published by the National Geographic Society. Apparently Bendavid-Val found all these black and white photographs in the archives of the State Museum of Tolstoy in 2000. So Sofya was actually taking a lot of photographs, and the implication of the review is that she saw her own artistic development in photography. What do you say about that?
Jay Parini: I knew that she was interested in photography, and it was of course a young form of art in those days. A lot of people around Tolstoy took pictures of him. This life was documented thoroughly. So it doesn't surprise me that Sofya was involved in taking pictures. I didn't know about this until recently, and I'd be very keen to see these pictures.

Ramona Koval: And it will be very interesting to see whether she saw herself as an artist.
Jay Parini: Her letters reveal a profoundly intelligent and sophisticated woman. Of course she knew all the intellectuals of the day, Anton Chekhov and others; they were always hanging around the house.

Ramona Koval: Although the acolytes around Tolstoy thought she wasn't fit to be the wife of a genius.
Jay Parini: But they worshiped Tolstoy, thought he was practically God. Nobody would have seemed appropriate in their eyes.

Ramona Koval: She accuses him of betraying her with his friend, Chertkov, suggesting he was a homosexual lover. What's the truth of that?
Jay Parini: Tolstoy, like a lot of great artists, was sexually omnivorous, and it's possible that he had slept with men in his youth—or had homoerotic feelings. It's not a surprise that she picked up on this. I doubt that he had any relations with Chertkov, however. She was jealous of him, that's all. This was paranoia on her part. She imagined things that didn't exist.

Ramona Koval: Chertkov doesn't sound like my idea of a nice bloke either.

Jay Parini: He was a puritan, a fierce, unrelenting, unhappy man who fixed on Tolstoy as a kind of savior, a religious leader. Tolstoy was surrounded by disciples.

Ramona Koval: And what were the features of being a Tolstoyan?
Jay Parini: First of all, you read the works of the master, and you memorized them. You leaned toward pacifism and vegetarianism—would never kill a living creature for food, and certainly not for political reasons. You identified with the peasantry. You have sex with preferably no one but certainly not outside of marriage. Tolstoyans were chaste.

Ramona Koval: How did they expect to procreate?
Jay Parini: It's sort of like the Shakers in New England; eventually they dwindled to the happy few, and then the unhappy fewer. There are no more Shakers.

Ramona Koval: They left a lot of chairs around.
Jay Parini: Nice furniture.

Ramona Koval: Tell me about Tolstoy's relationship with other greats of the age. You quote letters that he wrote to Ghandi and to George Bernard Shaw.
Jay Parini: Yes, Shaw and Gandhi both looked to Tolstoy for ideas, inspiration. Tolstoy was, in fact, a thinker with unusual capacities, turns of mind. His essays are very powerful. There's a book called *The Kingdom of God Is within You* that ranks, in my view, high among his achievements. He was also a shrewd critic.

Ramona Koval: He didn't much like Shakespeare, however.
Jay Parini: He considered Shakespeare a frivolous writer.

Ramona Koval: How did he get this idea?
Jay Parini: Shakespeare never promoted any obvious moral ideas. He made art for its own sake, although he subscribed to the Elizabethan world picture, and had his own notions of justice. Tolstoy disliked the concept of art for art's sake. He thought that writers should promote the social good, which is why his thinking prefigures Marxist-Leninist theories of art—art in service to the state. W. H. Auden used to play a funny game called "purgatory mates" and would imagine unlikely and incompatible people linking

arms as they marched through purgatory. I think he would have yoked Tolstoy with someone like Oscar Wilde. It would have been a very unpleasant journey for both of them.

Ramona Koval: They would have driven each other mad? Tolstoy was such a puritan and Oscar Wilde didn't take life seriously enough?
Jay Parini: That's right. Tolstoy would have hated those Wildean *bon mots*, witty remarks, his refusal to think about the poor. Tolstoy, to give him credit, really worried about the situation in Russia and the world. He hated state violence, having been in war himself, in the Caucasus. His pacifism was based on a knowledge of the cruelties, the absurdities, of war.

Ramona Koval: As he's dying, who are the authors that he's having read to him?
Jay Parini: Mainly Rousseau at the end. Tolstoy was very interested in educational theories. He reminds me of Wittgenstein, who went off to become an elementary school teacher in Norway after having been a world-class philosopher at Cambridge. Tolstoy started a school for young children, and he wrote textbooks for them. In the course of his life, Tolstoy also read everything. He was a hardworking guy, something of an autodidact. He taught himself Koine Greek in order to read the gospels in the original.

Ramona Koval: Let's talk about biography versus novels. You've written both.
Jay Parini: I began with John Steinbeck, then I did Robert Frost and, more recently, William Faulkner, but I've written two biographical novels. There's the one about Tolstoy, another focused on the life of Walter Benjamin, a German Jewish intellectual who was chased by the Nazis over the Pyrenees and committed suicide when he was caught.

Ramona Koval: Another flight novel.
Jay Parini: Yes, and another novel about an old intellectual at the end of life. A few of my friends think I'm excessively drawn to old men dying—especially old writers. But I'm generally interested in lives. The English biographer and novelist Peter Ackroyd is a very old friend. I once said, "Peter, you've written a dozen novels and you've written a dozen biographies (Dickens, T. S. Eliot, William Blake). What's the difference, would you say, between your novels and your biographies?" He replied, "In the novels I have to tell the truth but in the biographies I just make things up."

Ramona Koval: What does that really mean?

Jay Parini: That there is this thing called narrative. You're telling a story, whether you refer to the book as a biography or a novel. You have to select certain facts and repress others. You do this whether you're writing a biography or a novel. It's all storytelling.

Ramona Koval: Sure, but you have to make the choice about which path you want to go down. And what informs that choice? Is it a matter of what's available to you, or what tickles your imagination?

Jay Parini: You can get at truth more easily in a novel. For example, in *The Last Station* I have a scene towards the end where Sofya Tolstoy contemplates suicide. We know that on a certain day she threw herself into the pond on the property, hoping to drown herself. One of the servants saw this, and she was rescued. If you're writing a biography you can say no more than that, as the conventions of biography and scholarship won't allow you to move into her head. If you're writing a novel, you have the freedom to wander into her mind, to imagine her life, the circumstances that led her to the pond's edge, what she felt and thought as she plunged into the cold dark water.

Ramona Koval: In our last minute, Jay, was it a surprise for you to find out that the film was going to be made?

Jay Parini: Not really. When the novel came out, I had any number of film offers. I sold it to Anthony Quinn—Zorba the Greek. We became friends, and we worked together for years on versions of the script. He was about to make the movie when he died. It languished for several years, although I kept working with our producer, Bonnie Arnold, another good friend. We eventually got the script into the hands of Michael Hoffman, who rewrote it, then directed it. I worked closely with Mike, of course, and I visited the set during the filming in eastern Germany. It was a great deal of fun. I admire the final product.

Ramona Koval: Maybe Tolstoy is smiling on you, too.

Jay Parini: I hope he is. I've done whatever I could to remain true to his vision, at least in my novel. It's nevertheless a work of fiction, a shaped story, true to what I've been able to imagine about the last days of Tolstoy.

Jay Parini on *Why Poetry Matters*

Mitch Wertlieb / 2008

From Vermont Public Radio (June 6, 2008): http://www.vpr.net/news_detail/80854/vt-edition-interview-jay-parini-on-poetry-matters/. Reprinted by permission.

Mitch Wertlieb: We've been talking this hour about stories: characters, plots, and the joy of getting lost in books. The written word is no doubt a powerful medium, especially in the form of poetry. Jay Parini is a poet and professor at Middlebury College, and author of the new book, *Why Poetry Matters*. Jay, welcome back to *Vermont Edition*.
Parini: Mitch, it's good to be on your show again.

Wertlieb: The title of your book is a commentary in and of itself, and I wonder if you feel, from that title—that you feel that poetry needs to be defended, to some extent.
Parini: We live in a culture where people basically don't read poetry. People don't even understand why they should read poetry. A certain glaze comes over their eyes when they hear the word. So I do suspect that, in every age, poetry needs defending. Poets have been trying to defend their art since the time of Plato. But in a time of MTV and endless cable channels and iPads and such, I think poetry can easily get lost in the shuffle.

Wertlieb: Do you think people are maybe thinking about it the wrong way, though? Because I understand what you say when you—they hear the word "poetry," maybe they think of some of those classical poets, and a Shakespeare sonnet or something, that may not seem as relevant. But in some ways, isn't poetry all around us, even in some of those examples you just mentioned? I'm thinking about particularly well-written rap lyrics, let's say. I mean, isn't that a form of poetry, right there?
Parini: The irony is you see kids bopping along on the bus with their earphones on. They're experiencing genuine poetry every day. I know that I

62

listen to Bob Dylan frequently, and I consider that a real form of poetry. Poetry is lyric, a song lyric without the notes to distract you from the words. The ancient poets—Sappho and company—actually wrote their lyrics to be sung to the accompaniment of a lyre.

Wertlieb: There is some poetry, I think, even in something like a text message, that I think people might not be aware of, because you're taking out words, and you're having to use a sparser delivery message. I just wonder if people are writing poetry without realizing it sometimes.

Parini: Thomas Campion, an English poet from the seventeenth century, defined poetry as a system of linked sounds. There are lots of ways of linking sounds. Sometimes when you hear good political speakers—Barack Obama, Jessie Jackson, for instance—they're speaking in a kind of poetry. You listen to Martin Luther King's "I Have a Dream" speech, and that's pure poetry, making use of the techniques of poetry, including repetition, refrains, rhythms, words echoing other words, chimes, rhymes, internal rhymes.

Wertlieb: Why is it that you think poetry really matters when there's so much language in the marketplace?

Parini: Because poetry is language that conducts us toward the center of our experience as human beings. It's difficult to experience that when using the language of the marketplace: reading the newspapers, listening to the television. So you need the quiet of your room. You have to be sitting with a page in front of you. You read those words and turn them over slowly in your head, allowing yourself to be transported by carefully selected language, by language that rides a kind of internal music. You find yourself ushered into yourself, into the parts that matter.

Wertlieb: You use some wonderful examples throughout the book of people talking about the connections that poetry makes to the real world—again, why poetry matters. There's a quote from Wallace Stevens in your book that says, "There is always an analogy between nature and the imagination, and possibly poetry is merely the strange rhetoric of that parallel." I don't even think that Stevens meant that to be a poem, but it sounds almost poetic, the way he describes it, doesn't it?

Parini: Those lines of Stevens stay in the mind. Poets have a remarkable way of summoning concrete images from the air of abstraction, and putting an image in the head that stays there. It was W. H. Auden who described poetry as "memorable language." I like that definition as well as any other.

Wertlieb: And it can be simple, too. There is a very brief poem that you include in your book by Louise Glück, and she writes, "It is not the moon, I tell you.\ It is these flowers\ lighting the yard."

Parini: She's a wonderful poet, and she has an intimate sense of the natural world and its connections to the spirit. Emerson once suggested that nature is the symbol of the spirit, and that all natural facts are signs of spiritual facts. I think Glück understands this in a gut way. It animates her poems.

Wertlieb: Jay, why do you write poetry yourself?

Parini: Well, I've been writing poems for forty years now. It's what I do in the morning, what I think about when I wake up. I usually go to a coffee shop or to my study, early, and I begin my day by reading a poem. I often read one of my favorite poets: Louise Glück or Robert Hass, or Walt Whitman, Wordsworth, Robert Frost, Robert Penn Warren, Philip Levine, Charles Wright, Seamus Heaney, or Adrienne Rich. I have a bookshelf in my study where I keep the volumes by poets I especially admire. And often this reading gets me going. Writing is a response to reading. Every poem is a sequel to another poem, usually something I read long ago. I've always found writing poetry a way of paying attention to the world, a way to explore where I am at a particular moment—emotionally, spiritually, even politically. I never can tell where it's going to go, and most of the poems I write simply stay in my notebook in rough draft, fragmentary, incomplete. I let them lie there. Every so often, I go back and cull the best lines or half-written poems and revise them, finish them. Once in eight or ten years I publish a collection of the latest work. But publication is a way of getting rid of work, clearing the way for fresh poems.

Wertlieb: It occurs to me that your book, *Why Poetry Matters*, is timely in that you have been thrust into the news media recently. I need to ask you about this. You were teaching a course to some students on Robert Frost. These students were put in that class because they had vandalized a former Frost home. I wonder what that experience has been like for you, and have they responded to what you've taught them about Frost?

Parini: It horrified me that these kids trashed the Frost house in Ripton, a place that means a great deal to me. I go there often, for spiritual sustenance of a particular kind. One night the judge called and asked if I would donate my time to meet with the vandals, to teach them a little about Frost. I was skeptical, at first, but agreed. With some trepidation, I walked into this classroom and began by reading some poems of Frost. I read "Out, Out." I read "Fire and Ice." I read "The Road Not Taken." As I read, I could see the language working its magic on them. Frost spoke to these kids. This was part of the process of restoration, and actually, that's what poetry is. There's a great Hebrew phrase, *tikkun olam*: to repair the world. I think that, to some degree, poetry is language in the service of reparation. It's probably appropriate, in a peculiar way, that poetry should be used in a situation like this, used to bring these kids back to their truest selves, back into the community, through the use of communal language. I often think of that phrase by Adrienne Rich: "the dream of a common language." That's my dream. It's how I used poetry to make contact with these so-called vandals. They were only kids, and they did something stupid by breaking into his former house. I didn't want to blame them or punish them. I wanted to make contact with them, bring them face to face with the poetry of Frost. Let's call it poetic justice.

The Books That Changed America

Tom Ashbrook / 2008

From *On Point with Tom Ashbrook* (December 22, 2008): http://onpoint.wbur
.org/2008/12/22/books-that-changed-america. Reprinted by permission.

Ashbrook: From WBUR Boston, I'm Tom Ashbrook, and this is *On Point*. Thirteen books, one nation. Novelist and poet Jay Parini set out to list the key books that, he says, helped create the intellectual and emotional contours of this country. That is an invitation to argument, and to the question of what sway books still hold. But it's also just plain rich and fun. This hour *On Point*, thirteen books that shaped the country. You can join the conversation. Can the idea of this country, as it's evolved, be found in a baker's dozen books, and what would be on your list? Joining me now is Jay Parini, prolific novelist, critic, poet, and literary biographer. He's a professor of English and creative writing at Middlebury College in Vermont. He's written biographies of Frost, Faulkner, and Steinbeck—none of them made his list. His latest novel is *The Apprentice Lover*. His latest book of verse *The Art of Subtraction*. His list is at the heart of a new book, *Promised Land: Thirteen Books That Changed America*. Jay Parini, welcome to *On Point*.
Parini: Thank you, Tom, for having me on the show. It's good to be here.

Ashbrook: It's great to have you. I wish, before we go one step further, you'd just wing straight down your list. We'll talk about each, but just give us your list, straight up.
Parini: I begin with William Bradford's wonderful description of what happened with the pilgrims when they landed at Plymouth Rock—*Of Plymouth Plantation*. Then I go on to *The Federalist Papers* by the anonymous Publius, who was really Alexander Hamilton, James Madison, and John Jay—three of our Founding Fathers. Then I move into *The Autobiography of Benjamin Franklin*, one of my favorite books. I follow with *The Journals of Lewis and Clark*, the story of a spirited but arduous journey west to find the Northwest

Passage. Then I go on to *Walden*, Henry David Thoreau's account of living in his cabin by Walden Pond. Then I move to *Uncle Tom's Cabin*, the novel that stirred things up and got everybody in the north ready for the Civil War. After that, I tackle *Adventures of Huckleberry Finn*, which, remember, Hemingway called the great American book, the origin of our literature. He thought that all American writing derived from it. Then I turn to *The Souls of Black Folk*, a sequence of essays by W. E. B. Du Bois, the African American writer. His book was written in response to *Up from Slavery* by Booker T. Washington, which came out three years before. Then I turn to the book that gave me my title, *The Promised Land*—probably the least known book on my list. It's by Mary Antin, a Jewish woman from the Pale of Settlement who came to this country in the late nineteenth century on the great wave of immigration. She wrote this heartfelt, beautiful immigration memoir. After that I do *How to Win Friends and Influence People* by Dale Carnegie, a book that's meant a great deal to me personally, a genuinely useful book. And then I look at *The Common Sense Book of Baby and Childcare* by Dr. Spock. The last two books I examine are *On the Road*, Jack Kerouac's novel about the American counterculture, a Beat novel, and Betty Friedan's *The Feminine Mystique*, which got the second wave of feminism rolling.

Ashbrook:. Thirteen books: a baker's dozen. A baker's dozen that you say *in toto*, or individually, do what, exactly?
Parini: I tried to find books that helped to shape the nation's idea of itself, or maybe consolidate it, or defined a major trend. These books shifted American consciousness in a fresh direction, or redirected it. This is a protean nation. It's constantly reinventing itself. Change is where we live, although we have rough guidelines. These books reflect this shifting of American consciousness. Reading them, I began to find certain themes they shared, certain preoccupations. I may have located something of the American character here—the DNA of what it means to be an American.

Ashbrook: And let us pull it even closer to the claim you're making for these books, then: that they reflect a shift, or that they actually somehow changed or helped, themselves, change the country?
Parini: The process varies from book to book, but there's no doubt that each of these books, to some degree, consolidated an intellectual trend that was beginning to gather. Sometimes these authors simply caught the wave and rode it to its crest. Other times, they were right at the beginning, as with Betty Friedan. She was instrumental in maybe pulling the wheel on this

great ship of state and aiming the nose in a slightly different direction. But I make the point that not one of these books stands alone, that each of them represents a climate of opinion. Any number of books swirls in its wake. You couldn't have *Walden,* for instance, without first having the essays of Ralph Waldo Emerson; without having all the books written by the German romantic philosophers, or Wordsworth and Coleridge. *Walden* emerges from this gathering wave of thought. But then again, he opens up a new direction for American nature writing, one that's been followed by so many writers, right down to, say, *Pilgrim at Tinker Creek* by Annie Dillard.

Ashbrook: What about your title? It's Mary Antin's book title, *The Promised Land,* but you've also chosen it as your umbrella title for the thirteen books that changed America.
Parini: When I reread each of the thirteen books I finally chose to discuss, the phrase "promised land" often cropped up, from William Bradford to *On the Road.* In *On the Road,* the phrase "promised land" occurs many times. America was seen as a place of promise. Of course, it goes back to the idea of Moses leading the Israelites into the wilderness, and hoping to get to the promised land of Canaan. You get up to the mountain top, and you look and you see it. But it remains elusive.

Ashbrook: There it is. It's promised to you!
Parini: But it's never quite there. We're never going to get there. The promised land's always slightly out of our grasp. Imperfection is part of who we are. The Founding Fathers knew that even the U.S. Constitution of 1787 was hardly a perfect document. Working on *The Federalist Papers,* I came across one of the final speeches Ben Franklin himself gave, at the Philadelphia convention. He was a very old man and couldn't stand up and read the speech himself, so he got one of his best friends, James Wilson, to read it. And he says, "Look, I agree to this Constitution with all its faults, if they are such; because I think a general Government necessary for us, and there is no form of Government but what may be a blessing for the people if well administered, and I believe further that this is likely to be well administered for a course of years, and can only end in Despotism, as other forms have done before it, when the people shall become so corrupted as to need despotic Government, being incapable of any other." That note of caution sent a chill up my spine.

Ashbrook: Yes, indeed.

Parini: We think of the U.S. Constitution as something sacred. Myself, I get tired of hearing that we should always appoint strict constructionist judges to the Supreme Court because of our holy document. Thomas Jefferson himself suggested that every twenty years we'd have to revisit our constitution and do it over again. Each generation must have a chance to address these fundamental ideas, to make the necessary adjustments.

Ashbrook: I hear the insight and eloquence of Benjamin Franklin as you quote him there, and it brings a question to mind yet again, and we're going to dive into these books. But do you think these books still have sway? I mean, *Plymouth Plantation*? Lost for decades. *Federalist Papers*? Ripped straight out of the newspapers of their time. Do books still have the power to change, shape, influence this country? Or is that off to *Grand Theft Auto* and video games and I don't know what?
Parini: Let me just give you a little context, Tom. I spent a year abroad with my family in London. I sat there, three years ago, in the depths of the second term of George W. Bush. You know, my grandparents were immigrants from Italy. My parents never went to college. So I always believed that America was a hopeful place, with many opportunities. I saw America as the promised land. Only through access to good libraries and public schools did I finally manage to get an education, to become a professor and a writer, living the kind of life I wished for myself. Like millions of Americans, I owe a huge debt to this country. I've always been an optimistic person, proud of our fierce democratic tradition and our roots in the secular Enlightenment, which is what we are: an Enlightenment nation, created from whole cloth in the middle of the eighteenth century. So I was hopeful. Then I looked back over recent years, from the Vietnam War through the terrible years of the Bush administration; I saw this country dragged down by scoundrels. I had lost a lot of my enthusiasm about the American project, its grand promise. I began to reread our foundational texts, and suddenly I was on fire again for being an American. This country has always been a beacon on the hill, the famous and abused old phrase that politicians like to bend to their own purposes.

Ashbrook: Yep.
Parini: That phrase goes back to, you know, the Puritans. It's how Governor William Bradford saw the New World when the Separatists landed at Plymouth.

Ashbrook: Here's an excerpt from one book on Jay Parini's list. W. E. B. Du Bois's *The Souls of Black Folk*, read by Walter Covell. This is from the beginning, when he introduces the metaphor of the veil: the idea that African Americans have a special, private consciousness separate from mainstream society.

Covell Recording: "Leaving, then, the world of the white man, I have stepped within the Veil, raising it that you may view faintly its deeper recesses,—the meaning of its religion, the passion of its human sorrow, and the struggle of its greater souls."

Ashbrook: Just a note there from *The Souls of Black Folk*. Let's hear from a couple of our listeners, and then come to Jay. Harriet in Arlington, Massachusetts, you're on the air.

Harriet: *The Promised Land* by Mary Antin. I came across it by accident quite a while ago. I always wondered why it wasn't better known than Franklin's autobiography. I don't think a lot of people read it, but it's a lot of fun to read. So I wondered if you considered *Little Women*?

Parini: No, it's not in my list or even in my appendix, but it should be. I didn't put many novels on the list because I don't think novels—here I am, a novelist, saying this, and a poet, too—but I don't think novels and poems shift the culture in obvious ways.

Harriet: I can see that.

Parini: With *The Souls of Black Folk*, for example, we're talking about a book that really did define the terms of the racial debate in this country for the twentieth century. It was wildly prophetic. If you take Booker T. Washington's *Up from Slavery* (1900) and *The Souls of Black Folk* (1903), the debate unfolded in bold terms. It's a debate we're still having. To reread *The Souls of Black Folk* in the age of Obama . . . I found this thrilling. I went back to it a few weeks ago, reread it. It's so lovely, so shocking, as when he writes, "To be a poor man is hard, but to be a poor race in a land of dollars is the very bottom of hardship."

Ashbrook: And you're making choices at the same time. Harriet, thanks for your call. You're making choices right there, when you choose between Booker T. Washington and *The Souls of Black Folk*. Washington had a kind of milder view in *Up from Slavery*.

Parini: Yes, and a lot of the early essays of Du Bois take direct issue with *Up from Slavery*, saying to us: Look, we can't have this mild approach. Du Bois wrote, "Mr. Washington represents, in Negro thought, the old attitude of adjustment and submission." I love that phrase: adjustment and submission. What I admire in Du Bois is the fiery note. When Barack Obama's says "Yes, we can," he has got Du Bois behind him, saying, "We really, really can, and we will." We shall overcome, as the old song goes. That note of confident protest, of defiance and pride, first appears in Du Bois.

Ashbrook: Let's go to American Falls, Idaho, and Todd.
Todd: Yes, thank you both. I enjoy your program very much. The word "promised land" prompted me to give you a call. The reason is that in your discussion, you mentioned *Promised Land* in your thirteen books. I just want to express to you that there's one other book that mentions the word "promised land." It mentions it 2,113 times.

Ashbrook: And that book is?
Todd: *The Book of Mormon.*

Ashbrook: A very American book if there ever was one.
Todd: There are 140 million copies of that book in print.

Ashbrook: It's on your list of a hundred further books to read, Jay.
Parini: Yes, of course. I was just out in Utah giving a talk at Sundance, in the land of Mormons. My wife's family were Mormons, on her mother's side, and I have read *The Book of Mormon.* The first question that arose after my talk was this: "What about *The Book of Mormon*?" And I said it was an authentic American religious text. Only Mary Baker Eddy and Joseph Smith wrote authentic visionary books—books that shaped the American religious experience. And if you read through *Promised Land,* you will hear that high religious note. But we're a secular country, created by a group of guys—remember, there were no women in those days—by a group of guys sitting in Philadelphia who forged this marvelous constitution.

Ashbrook: No women in the hall, right?
Parini: No women. Women don't come fully or politically into view until the nineteenth amendment, in 1920, when they finally got to vote, or maybe at the Seneca Falls Convention of 1848, when they gathered to begin agitating for women's rights. But the note of a promised land, which is a religious idea, sounds from the beginning. When the Separatists came on the *Mayflower,* they brought with them a large hopefulness. They were religious

people. *Of Plymouth Plantation*, Bradford's memoir, is a deeply religious book. Even our secular writers, as in *Walden*, filled with religious thought and feeling. Thoreau was activated by the spirit. This is a deeply religious country—that is simply the case—but it's a country which, constitutionally, is a secular entity. This allows people to follow their inner lights without interference from the state. That's a key part of our tradition.

Ashbrook: *The Book of Mormon* makes the greater list of a hundred further books in your appendix. So does Reinhold Niebuhr's *Moral Man and Immoral Society*. Todd, thank you for calling. Jay, let's dive in. *Of Plymouth Plantation* by Bradford, who was governor there. You remind us of our whole image that later informed Abraham Lincoln's notion of Thanksgiving and the country more broadly comes very much out of the pages of this book, which turned out to be a long, lost text.

Parini: Bradford had the advantage of historical access. He was the governor of the plantation for decades. He wrote this vivid journal that concerns the establishment of the colony at Plymouth Rock. It was mysteriously lost after his death—lost for three centuries. An American tourist discovered the manuscript in London in 1850. He copied it by hand, and it was published in 1856. Abraham Lincoln read it during the height of the Civil War: the fact that the early pilgrims managed to get along with the Indians had relevance. Lincoln declared Thanksgiving a national holiday in 1863, a time of great difficulty for the nation. Americans don't know this, usually. As Gore Vidal said, we are the United States of Amnesia. One of the things I tried to do for this amnesiac country in *Promised Land* is supply memory. You know, when you're talking to somebody who has Alzheimer's, you often supply memory for them, in order to have a conversation. That's what I do in each of these essays, filling in America's wonderful, complex history, and also its myth-making. Lincoln, in declaring Thanksgiving a national holiday, created a founding myth. That's what so many of these key texts do. They create myths we can live by.

Ashbrook: There's a couple of books that echo one another here. *The Autobiography of Benjamin Franklin* and then *How to Win Friends and Influence People*, long after . . . What do you see each of them standing for in your lineup?

Parini: In a nutshell: Ben Franklin created the American character. He also invented the genre of autobiography. Before Franklin there were memoirs by statesmen, or saints' lives. But no average person said, "Here's how I created myself." That's what Franklin did. He listed things you must do: you must be chaste, you must be diligent, you must work hard, stay up late at night, whatever it takes to be successful. Dale Carnegie comes along in the midst of the Great Depression, in 1936, and publishes this inspiring book: *How to Win Friends and Influence People*, drawing heavily on Ben Franklin. He said, "Look, you have it in your own hands to pick yourself up, and to make something of yourself; to get ahead in your life." Of course, it instructs you how to become a good salesman. One of the little details I came across was that since Glasnost—since the fall of Communism in Russia—this book has been published in twenty-eight different editions in Russia alone. The book appeals to people who want to make it on their own, to get their lives under control.

Ashbrook: But it's often dissed as a book that promotes insincerity.
Parini: Well, there is that. I talk about this in the book. It also creates the how-to book. I spent a few weeks reading things like *The Purpose Driven Life*, which I found inspiring. Some of these inspirational books put me off, however. Joel Osteen, for instance. I don't have much time for the so-called prosperity gospel. That notion reflects the darker side of Benjamin Franklin—you know, the power of positive thinking: "You're going to get ahead in this life, fella, and you damn well better!" Also, the puritan idea that God shines His light on those who succeed. Therefore, if you happen to be, say, handicapped, or poor, or have been born in unfortunate circumstances, there's not much hope for you, buddy. Sorry about that. You get a little bit of that in Dale Carnegie, but there's a lot inspiring here, too. He says in his first chapter, "If you want to make friends, find something good in everybody around you, and make it known to them. Talk to them." And so, I do talk to them. Actually, when I was a thirteen- to fourteen-year old in middle school . . .

Ashbrook: You did it!
Parini: I did. I was a very shy boy from Scranton, PA. I had no friends—that's how it felt. I was very, very shy. So I looked around my classroom, got a notebook, and put everybody's name down, one after the other. I found something to compliment in each kid. There was a fellow who was an amazing football player. He could throw beautiful passes. I remember waiting for the right moment, and I said, "You have a great arm. How do you throw passes like that?" That guy stuck with me through high school. We became real friends. There was one girl I felt sorry for her. There was nothing going

for this girl, shall we just say. I won't describe her. In an introductory Spanish class, I heard her say the word *burro*. And I'd never heard that roll before. It's as if there were fourteen *r*'s—.

Ashbrook: A full trill, right.

Parini: She could roll that *r*. So I went up to her and said, "Lydia, the way you pronounce those words in that Spanish class, you could be almost, you know, like, Spanish." She would have married me that day.

Ashbrook: You've got another pairing on here, in a way: two journeys, one long and one more intimate. *The Journals of Lewis and Clark* sits on your list next to *Walden*.

Parini: The expedition of Lewis and Clark represents one of the great American stories. With the Louisiana Purchase, Jefferson had suddenly doubled the size of the United States of America. He wondered—everybody wondered—what could be found in this vast territory? Was there a way to get from St. Louis up to the northwest frontier by river? Jefferson commissioned Meriwether Lewis and William Clark to set off on this journey of exploration, and they started in 1803 on this journey of twenty-eight months that was quite extraordinary. They record the details in their voluminous journals, which have in every generation been re-edited, re-presented to the American public. One of the things I do in *Promised Land* is track the publication history of each book, noting how often they spoke to different audiences at different times. Every twenty years or so there has been a new edition of Lewis and Clark. Each edition reflects the concerns of the particular time in which it appears.

Ashbrook: Can you describe the change to American culture it provoked— in contrast with *Walden*?

Parini: Nicholas Biddle, in 1814, brought out an edition which was a huge bestseller. And what did it do? It started a wave of immigration. Suddenly westward expansion began in earnest. People read *The Journals of Lewis and Clark* and packed their bags, sold their houses, and headed west. They began settling the new territories. In "The Gift Outright," Robert Frost has that great phrase: "A land vaguely realizing westward." That's what for decades we saw: this nation—sometimes peacefully, sometimes violently—occupying the land to the west of the Mississippi. Let's turn to *Huck Finn*, another great journey, in this context. Mark Twain asks us to rethink what freedom means at every bend in the river. He invites us to believe in the powers of invention, to celebrate in the cockeyed world of boyhood. He presses us to erase the boundaries of class and color that, you know, keep us in our separate spheres, and he urges us to explore the, you know, depth of pleasure that nature at every turn in the river offers. Needless to say, he does this with his wonderful wry sense of humor—Twain is so wonderful that way. And it still seems peculiarly American to me, this voice he creates. He provides at every turn—even rereading *Huckleberry Finn*, which I do so regularly—an antidote to the kind of pompous, self-important rubbish that, you know, fills our newspapers and magazines, and, you know, clogs the airwaves most days. Not you, Tom.

Ashbrook: Thanks, Jay.
Parini: You're a refreshing exception to what I just said.

Ashbrook: Here's Jack Kerouac himself reading from his novel, *On the Road.*
Kerouac Recording: "So Dean and I raced on to the East Coast. At one point we drove a 1947 Cadillac limousine across the state of Nebraska 110 miles an hour, beating hot-shot passenger trains and steel-wheel freights in one nervous, shuddering snap up of the gas. We told stories and zoomed East. There were hobos by the tracks, wino bottles, the moon shining on wood fires. There were white-faced cows out in the plains, dim as nuns."

Ashbrook: "Dim as nuns," he said. Let's get a call from Andover, in Connecticut. Tom, you're on the air with Jay Parini.
Tom: I'm calling about Kerouac. I was, as a teenager growing up in New York, one of the generation influenced by Kerouac, and I am still, to this day, influenced by him. I went to see the scroll—I guess that would be my Holy Grail—opened up wide, in the New York Library in Manhattan earlier this year. I was just wondering why you chose this book.
Parini: I suspect that more than one generation of readers has found in *On the Road* an appealing mood of rebelliousness, an attitude, a way of being in the world. The exuberance of youth shines through these pages. The hipsters in Kerouac's novel live at breakneck speed. Sal Paradise: just think of the name of the main character. He's searching for paradise on earth. He is the ultimate American quester, living in opposition to his parents' culture. You can easily see how *On the Road* appealed to the burgeoning hippy generation. I come from that generation, and I found all of this attractive. But Kerouc goes back, of course, to the hipsters of the fifties and the late

forties. He was present at the creation of the counterculture, though there had been, of course, a fringe culture way before that. Kerouac—in a paradoxical move—kind of mainstreams the counterculture. That sounds like an oxymoron. He's writing about a tribe of people. They're living in an ecstasy of perpetual movement. They refuse to abide by the sexual mores of their parents. They break the sexual boundaries, sleeping with a lot of different women. Homosexuality surfaces in this novel, especially in its early version. It's very explicit. But the novel is also about the search for God, what Kerouac calls "it." Sal Paradise wants to find "it," even "Him," God. But his characters don't seek the Divine in conventional ways, not in churches. They're more like Emerson and Thoreau, who went into the mountains, the church of the woods. Kerouac's young men find God in a desert landscape. They find God in the prairies, in the jazz clubs of San Francisco.

Ashbrook: Typed first on a scroll, the book makes your short list, the thirteen. Let's get a call from Joshua. Tom, thanks for calling. Let's go to Hartford, Connecticut. Joshua. You're on the air, Joshua.
Joshua: Hi, Tom and Jay. Thanks for taking my call.

Ashbrook: Yeah.
Joshua: Jay, I want to know how close Walt Whitman's *Leaves of Grass* came to being on this list. It seems to me a massively influential book that anticipates, in many important ways, everything you just said about Kerouac.
Parini: A great question. And I have to say the hardest book to leave off this list was *Leaves of Grass*. I will say this: no book of poetry in America means more to me. It's a book I teach year after year. As Tom has mentioned, I've been writing poems myself for some forty years. Poetry matters to me. So I put *Leaves of Grass* on my 100 more books that changed America. But you'd have to admit that very few people read *Leaves of Grass* when it was published in the middle of the nineteenth century. A century later it had become important, especially for American poets, even for novelists such as Kerouac. If I had a fourteenth book in *Promised Land*, it would probably be *Leaves of Grass*.

Ashbrook: They may not have been reading Walt Whitman at the time of its writing or near after, but they were sure reading Harriet Beecher Stowe. And *Uncle Tom's Cabin* does make your list. She was given credit by Abraham Lincoln for the war.
Parini: In 1863 Lincoln welcomed Harriet Beecher Stowe to the White

House. He said to her, with a touch of whimsy: "So you're the little lady that started this great war." That's an exaggeration, but it's true enough that she consolidated abolitionist sentiment in the North. From the time this book was published—in 1852—there were eight presses running day and night, churning out copies. Only the Bible sold more copies to readers in America than *Uncle Tom's Cabin* in the whole of the nineteenth century. This is the one book of the thirteen that, frankly, I'd never read before. I always assumed that it was a trashy novel that was nevertheless influential. One Saturday morning I started reading. I read through until midnight—the whole book in one day. This novel is Stephen King on steroids. Stowe is a storyteller to beat the band.

Ashbrook: But Stephen King doesn't make your list, and she does, as an author having written a book that changed the country, by your estimations.
Parini: True. Let me say that I've read a lot of Stephen King's novels. But no, he doesn't make my list. Much as I love King—and I do—he doesn't make my list.

Ashbrook: But *Uncle Tom's Cabin* does, and in a very big way. Rod is calling from Watertown, Massachusetts. Hi, Rod, you're on the air.
Rod: I would like the author to reflect a little bit on the book that is on the more feminine side, which is *The Feminine Mystique*. I would like to hear what he thinks of that book, and what kind of influence that book has on our society.
Parini: As I've said, each of these books has a long back story. It exists within a stream, swirls in a climate of opinion. Betty Friedan has before her all that's been happening for over a century with women trying to get the vote, looking for a place in society. After the excitement of getting the vote in 1920, there was a lull. Women shuffled back into the kitchen, into the nursery room. Then came World War II. Women—Rosie the Riveter—emerged again, working to promote the war effort. They felt useful. After the war, the men came rushing home, covered in glory. Women were pushed back into the home, and some of them didn't like their new position. Betty Friedan caught the second wave of feminism perfectly. The first wave would be the suffragettes, getting the vote for women. The second wave was when Betty Friedan, and the writers that swirl around her, said, "Okay. We're not happy. Something is wrong. Men are running this society. We have no voice, no place in the world." In *The Feminine Mystique*, Friedan laid out the landscape for feminism in such a powerful way. This was, remember, published

in, what, 1964? Around the time of the Civil Rights Act. And for the first time, discrimination—.

Ashbrook: 1963.
Parini: Right. There was a huge debate in the U.S. Congress about racial discrimination. But what about discrimination based on sex or gender? It was a big deal when the law finally said you couldn't discriminate on these counts. *The Feminine Mystique* sold millions of copies in the wake of that excitement, setting off what I think is one of the great shifts in American society. This is a book that helped to push the second wave of feminism, to push women back into the workplace, suggesting that women should have equal pay for equal work. As Friedan points out, it was actually about the liberation of men as well. Men had lost touch with their children, with their families. This division of labor in the household created a wall of isolation that was not good for the men, not good for the women, and certainly not good for the children. Betty Friedan was not an original thinker. I won't go that far. Most of her ideas were taken from Simone de Beauvoir and other feminist theoreticians. But she was a wonderful consolidator, a village explainer. She wrote in a vivid way. Anyone can still benefit from rereading this book.

Ashbrook: *The Feminine Mystique*, number thirteen on Jay Parini's list of thirteen. Jay, reel us back to *The Promised Land* and Mary Antin. As you say, this was an immigrant from—what, old Russia?—from the Pale of Settlement, the Jewish *shtetl*. She came first to Boston, and then on from there. The immigrant experience was at the forefront of her life and her book.
Parini: Antin's book occupies one of the great genres of American writing—the immigrant memoir. I could have chosen any one of twenty or thirty that I admired. Everybody who came to this country during the great wave of immigration from southern Italy, like my grandparents, or from the Pale of Settlement, or from Czechoslovakia, or anywhere from, say, Slavic countries. In fact, everybody in this country who is not a Native American is an immigrant, and a fairly recent immigrant. Even the first real settlers in the sixteenth century were immigrants from Europe. There were a lot of Spanish immigrants, too. They were here very early on. French immigrants, German, Dutch immigrants were here with the English settlers who came with the Puritans. So this is by no means a white, Anglo-Saxon country. But I chose Mary Antin because her book, published in 1912, defined the immigrant experience in classic terms, offering a paradigm. The boot of

the law was on the neck of Mary Antin's family in the Pale of Settlement. As Jews, they experienced pogroms. They couldn't travel outside the Pale without special permission. And they heard rumors about this marvelous place called America. My own grandmother recalled her own passage in 1912, from Italy, in steerage. A lot of people died en route, with burials at sea. As a child, I heard those stories and was amazed to come across it again in Antin's book—almost the same words. Many people died on Antin's difficult passage. She came in the 1890s. She and her family arrived in this country with huge expectations; but far from seeing the streets of gold, they were tossed together with a lot of poor families in the slums of Boston. The immigrant groups struggled: Irish against Italians, the Italians against the Jews, Jews against the Russians, against Poles, everybody trying to get a foothold, to rise up. Through the use of public libraries and schools—the wonders of the American public school system—she got her education. She was an astonishingly gifted writer. I would defy anyone to read *The Promised Land* and not see splendor in her writing.

Ashbrook: Jay, our time grows so short. I have to ask you if these books still hold the same sway in a period where an awful lot of folks are kind of checking out from books—you know, have moved on to movies, or video games. Do books still have that same influence?

Parini: I'll say two things. First of all, everybody listening to this radio program has been shaped by these books, and more books, even if they haven't read the books. That's because these books have shaped America's character, and we inherit that character at the moment of birth. Our society was forged by thinkers of considerable weight and originality. Second, I think it's a mistake to think books will die because they must compete with more popular media. Reading is thinking. Writing is thinking. As long as people breathe, they're going to read books, and they're going to want to return to the touchstone of great works.

After Words: Jay Parini, *Promised Land*

Sam Tanenhaus / 2008

Transcribed from C-SPAN Book TV, *After Words*, with Sam Tanenhaus, Editor, *New York Times Book Review*, which was taped on December 8, 2008, and aired on February 6, 2009. Copyright © 2008 by C-SPAN. http://www.youtube.com/watch?v=47MROw4LMOs.

Tanenhaus: Welcome to Book TV's *After Words*. I'm here with Jay Parini, prolific author, also professor of English. You've written a new book called *Promised Land: Thirteen Books That Changed America.* How did you come to write this book?

Parini: I was living in London a few years ago, and one night—it was a hot summer night in Hampstead—my wife said, "There's a talk down the street. Lord Melvyn Bragg is going to talk about the twelve books that changed the world." I didn't want to go, but she dragged me to it, and I'm grateful to her for that. There was a large audience, and Bragg's book on the topic was a big bestseller. It turned out all of his choices were English books. Patriotism overwhelmed me. I thought, "Well, what would be the twelve books that changed America, whatever change means?" I began scribbling in the margin some possibilities. I finally wound up with thirteen, and I thought it was analogous with the thirteen colonies. I just couldn't boil it down beyond the thirteen. I felt I needed an immigration memoir as one of these books, and I put in Mary Antin's *The Promised Land.* That gave me my title: *Promised Land.* This was during the late days of the Bush administration. Well, not late enough.

Tanenhaus: Did you think of these as bedrock books? The thirteen?

Parini: A good question. These are not the thirteen *greatest* books. I wouldn't even dream of going there. I won't even say "The thirteen books that changed America." Just "Here are thirteen books that really did have an impact." In fact, I should have called the book *Thirteen Books That Shaped America*, rather than "changed."

Tanenhaus: Well, what do you mean by "change" in this context?

Parini: These books serve as landmarks for certain intellectual traditions in the culture. I was trying to take an X-ray of the American psyche. These thirteen books helped to build this thing called the American character. And we do have a character. More than we know it, we've been shaped by the books that we've read, books that have seeped into the unconscious.

Tanenhaus: So one thing you've done is cover a really long timespan. You go back to the beginning. Let's start with some of the books. Your first one is *Of Plymouth Plantation*. Tell us a little bit about that one. It has an unusual history.

Parini: That was part of the fun for me. I thought, "Where do you begin a book about America?" Well, the pilgrim landing at Plymouth Rock seemed a right place to begin. William Bradford, still a young man, was elected governor by his cohorts, and he governed for decades, presiding over the Plymouth Colony. *Of Plymouth Plantation*—in its manuscript form—disappeared for hundreds of years, after Bradford's death. Remember, the Pilgrims landed in 1620, and Bradford was working on this book up until 1647, when it breaks off. It tells the wonderful story of how the Pilgrims got along with local Wampanoag Indians, among other things. The journal was discovered centuries later by a traveler in England.

Tanenhaus: When was this?

Parini: In the middle of the nineteenth century.

Tanenhaus: Was the diary known of during the time it was missing? Was it something people were looking for?

Parini: Some of the early Pilgrim Fathers mentioned the diaries, even quoting passages. People knew it had existed, and wondered where it was. It was a huge literary discovery.

Tanenhaus: So this was a book that shaped America long after it was written.

Parini: I think so. What I suggest is all of these thirteen books are myth-making books. Every culture has stories of its own origins, for instance. The Roman Empire had the tale of Romulus and Remus. But the story of Plymouth Plantation is one of our founding myths. Myths are not necessarily true stories, but they're stories that have a shaping power. The story of the Pilgrims landing on Plymouth Rock, surviving the first winter, getting help from the local tribe of Native Americans, and the whole politics of the Plymouth Colony are fascinating, part of every American's psyche. We learn this stuff in elementary school.

Tanenhaus: Now, another book you write about, which our viewers will be very aware of, is *The Federalist Papers*. In a sense, they weren't really a book at all.

Parini: I first read this collection of essays in college. It's stayed in my mind all this time—a luminous book, which I've dipped into throughout my life. It's written by Publius—a *nom de plume* chosen by John Jay, Alexander Hamilton, and James Madison. They wrote these eighty-five individual essays, ad hoc, to try to convince Americans to ratify the new proposed U.S. Constitution.

Tanenhaus: Where were these essays published?

Parini: In New York newspapers—largely to convince New Yorkers to get behind the proposed constitution. The essays were disseminated throughout the thirteen colonies, and they played a part in marshaling opinion. Remember, there was a huge anti-federalist movement, with people like George Mason, after whom George Mason University is founded, arguing that the U.S. Constitution was an incredibly bad idea, a flawed document. There was a pamphleteer called Federal Farmer, someone who wrote under that pseudonym, arguing that the rights of states would be jeopardized if the new constitution went into effect, and that civil liberties would be destroyed.

Tanenhaus: We don't know who he was, right?

Parini: No, we don't. Richard Henry Lee was often put forward as a name, but that has been questioned by recent historians. There were a lot of anti-federalists, and the debate raged. Americans forget how much this was up for grabs, the U.S. Constitution.

Tanenhaus: What were the main issues of contention when the Constitution was written, ratified, and when these founders were quarreling about it?

Parini: The Articles of Confederation was in effect beforehand, and it gave to states immense powers of self-government. The states would now have to concede an awful lot of independence to the federal government. This frightened many. Democracy scared some, too. What if the mob took control of the nation? Remember, democracy was in its infancy, a new thing in the world. The French Revolution was only beginning, although we stole many of our ideas from French thinkers. One of the things I say about *The Federalist Papers* is how lucky we were that our founding fathers were so well educated. They had read the Greek and Roman historians and political philosophers. They had studied Montesquieu and Voltaire. As you read through these essays, your jaw drops at the range of allusion, the sophistication of the rhetoric. This is classical rhetoric—rhetoric is the art of persuasion—taken to the nth power. These elegant essays defend the federal system as put forward in the U.S. Constitution, with its separation of powers, a bicameral legislature with power generally distributed in various (even curious) ways among the three branches of government.

Tanenhaus: Issues that are very much with us today, particularly during the Bush years.
Parini: Well, one of the great controversies that arose at the convention was how much power we should give to the president to make war. There was tremendous opposition to giving the president too much power to act on his own.

Tanenhaus: How many of their concerns were based on their own experiences as colonists ruled by a monarch?
Parini: They thought seriously about how much authority a king had, and one of the questions was, "Should we turn the president into a king?" One notion was that we should have three presidents, in fact. An unwieldy prospect.

Tanenhaus: Three at once?
Parini: That's right. There was controversy about how long the president should stay in power, too. Some thought the presidency should not be limited in the number of terms. There was some concern about having any number of strange ghosts, our ex-presidents, wandering around the capital and causing trouble. The Supreme Court was another issue debated fiercely in *The Federalist Papers*, just as it was debated in Philadelphia. The idea that the president should be able to nominate judges terrified some, who worried that a future president could stack the deck at the Supreme Court.

Tanenhaus: Which some would say has happened.

Parini: Yes. In reading *The Federalist Papers*, I marveled at how current they seemed, and how so many of the problems, potential flaws, issues being raised were things debated at this moment. Nothing could be more relevant to our situation now as we rethink the American future than *The Federalist Papers*.

Tanenhaus: They foresaw a great deal, as you mentioned. What didn't they foresee?

Parini: The issue of slavery is never mentioned once. I think this was a conscious elision. Nobody wanted to discuss it.

Tanenhaus: Why?

Parini: Many of the Founding Fathers, such as Thomas Jefferson, were slave owners. It was awkward.

Tanenhaus: Of course, this became contentious almost a century later when many debates about slavery revolved around the fact that there wasn't really any mention of it in the founding document.

Parini: Yes. That's right. I reread the Constitution before I reread *The Federalist Papers*. It's a very slim document, without elaboration. Essentially *The Federalist Papers* had to flesh it out. It's interesting that, for instance, there's no such phrase "the separation of powers" in the Constitution. This goes back to *The Federalist Papers*, although many future Supreme Court Justices refer to the Constitution's supposed doctrine of the separation of powers.

Tanenhaus: How did they come up with the term "president"? In etymological terms, it means "someone who presides." Now, was that a way of saying he won't be an all-powerful dictator or monarch?

Parini: There was a lot of concern that the president of the United States should simply be the person who executes the laws of the people. The president does not make the laws, he presides. He is *primus inter pares*, right? First among equals.

Tanenhaus: First among equals.

Parini: That was a crucial idea put forward in *The Federalist Papers*. The president is not the king. The people retain the right to overthrow him and his cabinet.

Tanenhaus: And their own government.

Parini: It's there, the right to overthrow our government if it ever becomes tyrannical. It seems important to recall that our Founding Fathers were liberal-minded, Enlightenment intellectuals. They had read John Locke, David Hume, and Voltaire. They were not Christians, for the most part. They were Deists. And some of them were fairly remote Deists, like Benjamin Franklin.

Tanenhaus: Franklin's *Autobiography* is another book on your list. I wonder if our viewers realize just how important his book is. You say it's really the first of all modern autobiographies. Why is that?

Parini: Franklin invented many things: bifocal lenses, the catheter, batteries to store electricity. He invented the Franklin stove. He created matching funds, and he founded libraries as well as the University of Pennsylvania. But most people don't realize he invented the genre of autobiography.

Tanenhaus: What sets this one apart?

Parini: Autobiography, as conceived by Franklin, is really about the creation of the self on the page. This tradition begins with Franklin.

Tanenhaus: And how does Franklin describe it? Through episodes from his life? Through people he met and knew? His career? All these things?

Parini: He creates a persona. And in creating that persona—persona is a mask—he created the American character. The American character is a man like Franklin, who comes from nowhere.

Tanenhaus: Where did he come from?

Parini: A poor family in Boston. His father made soap. Franklin took a job with one of his older brothers as an apprentice printer, but he didn't get along with him, so at the age of seventeen, he escaped from Boston. His parents were afraid he had run away to sea. In fact, he did go to sea, but only to Philadelphia. And he landed—he tells this story—with three loaves of bread, walked up Market Street in Philadelphia with these under his arm. He met a poor woman with a little child, and he gave them two of his three loaves. That's a symbolic moment. In due course, he established a printing house that became a major publishing firm. Then he wrote *Poor Richard's Almanac*, with its famous sayings.

Tanenhaus: Don't put off until tomorrow what you can do today.

Parini: Exactly. Early to bed, early to rise, / Makes a man healthy, wealthy, and wise. This is Old Ben. With his sayings, he creates the American character.

Tanenhaus: And yet, there are some who were very skeptical of this virtuous American that Franklin described. For instance, the great English novelist D. H. Lawrence was very skeptical.
Parini: In his study of classic American literature, he regarded Franklin as a moral prig. Even a number of Americans, such as Emerson, held a negative view of Franklin. Herman Melville considered Franklin as shallow as dishwater.

Tanenhaus: Why did they think this?
Parini: Because he's so concerned with getting ahead in life. He seems utterly focused on the surfaces of life: how to make money; how to further your business interests. There is a part of Franklin's character which is a little unsavory. He flattered people, his bosses especially, to get ahead.

Tanenhaus: He describes this in the autobiography?
Parini: It's between the lines. In the course of the book, he puts across the story of his success, saying: "Look at me. I was a poor boy from Boston. I came down to Philadelphia with nothing. Within a very few years, I owned my own printing shop. Soon I was a central player on the American scene." He's our perfect Rotarian—the man in a leather apron who's doing his best for society. He never contemplates the motions of his soul. There's not a religious bone in Franklin's body, though for a brief period he had some interest in a preacher he had befriended, but that fell away quickly. Later in life, of course, he went off to become our ambassador to Paris. His life grew larger and larger.

Tanenhaus: This "prig" was lionized in Paris, wasn't he?
Parini: They called him "the American Voltaire," and he liked to dine with beautiful women, with lords and ladies. He dressed elegantly. He drank crates of wine. When John Adams joined Franklin in Paris in 1779, he wrote back in horror. He said, in essence: "This old man is a reprobate. He's drunk every night. He's chasing after women, and he's a man in his seventies!" Franklin was a practical man, of course, and a great ambassador. When in France, do as the French. They loved him. And we owe a great deal to Franklin for all the wine he drank, as he forged a crucial alliance with France during the American Revolution. Later, he negotiated the Treaty of Paris, after

the Revolutionary War. This was in 1783, and it ended the Revolutionary War. Franklin was, perhaps, the greatest American.

Tanenhaus: We've talked about the colonial period, which was really limited to one segment, the east coast of the United States. But you've also included *The Journals of Lewis and Clark*. Now we enter the age of exploration. How did that book come to be written?
Parini: One of our foundational stories involves westward expansion: Manifest Destiny. This book was a result of an exploratory mission by the Corps of Discovery, as it was called. Thomas Jefferson sent this small band, under the leadership of Lewis and Clark, on their way westward.

Tanenhaus: And who were Lewis and Clark?
Parini: Two former soldiers. Meriwether Lewis had been a secretary to Thomas Jefferson, and he was friendly with William Clark. The territory in question was vast, of course. And there were no reliable maps of the region. One heard rumors of a river that went all the way to the Pacific—a mythical river. One of the main reasons for the expedition was to create maps, to convey a sense of the geography of the region we had just purchased, and to find out about the people who lived there. Who exactly were all these Native Americans? What were they like? Were they dangerous? Also, commerce played a role. We wanted to get our hands on whatever natural resources were there: furs, timber . . . whatever we could find.

Tanenhaus: When did it happen? When did they begin their expedition?
Parini: They set off in 1804 and were gone for roughly two years. And it was one hell of a journey. The journals make for good reading.

Tanenhaus: How big a book are we talking about?
Parini: I believe I have eight volumes in my edition.

Tanenhaus: And that's how they were published and read at the time?
Parini: No, they were nearly always published in excerpts. Every generation, a new editor would make a fresh selection, pitching the journey in a different way. For example, during the Cold War, there was an edition that makes Lewis and Clark into early astronauts. There's a strong nationalistic thread that runs through some editions. This is a do-it-yourself kit, the journals of Lewis and Clark. It's an extraordinary tale. Of course, they were helped along the way. It's also a story of how to get along with people. The Indi-

ans were rightfully skeptical of these strange foreigners arriving in canoes. These white men had these rifles that would kill. Nevertheless, the Corps of Discovery could never have gotten to Oregon and back without the help of lots of different tribes.

Tanenhaus: You have three classics, three great American classics—all very different—all about the great, peculiar institution, and the problem of race in America. Which books did you choose?
Parini: Well, there's *Uncle Tom's Cabin* by Harriet Beecher Stowe, the book that mobilized antislavery sentiment in the North.

Tanenhaus: Published when?
Parini: In 1852, and it was a huge bestseller. The novel was vastly popular throughout the world. You can't begin to imagine the number of sales. Harriet Beecher Stowe became a major world figure.

Tanenhaus: Who was she?
Parini: Just a quiet, intellectual girl from a religious family from Ohio. Her father was a preacher. Her brother became a very famous preacher and theologian. She was a housewife who had written a few stories, and she sent a sample chapter of this book she wanted to write to an abolitionist newspaper. The editor wrote back and said, "Please, give us a whole novel. We love it." It was published first in this form, and it took off.

Tanenhaus: Now, at this time, many people in the North really didn't know much about slavery. How did she learn so much?
Parini: She crossed over the border to a plantation in Kentucky a couple of times. The abolition movement engaged her, and she met a lot of runaway slaves. She heard from them such horrific tales about how cruelly slaves were treated. We forget sometimes how terrible the suffering was of American slaves. Toni Morrison in her novel *Beloved* has a memorable dedication: "To the sixty million dead." They died in slavery. The dehumanization of human beings was appalling: turning people into property. Husbands were separated from wives. Children from parents. The extent of the cruelty could vary from plantation to plantation. That is, there were many "good" slave owners who treated their slaves well. Nevertheless, as an institution, it was horrible, immoral.

Tanenhaus: And what is the story?

Parini: It's a narrative about a wonderful, beautiful, innocent slave girl called Eliza. She learns that she's being separated from her young family. Her husband is taken away from her, and she is sold elsewhere. The separation is painful. Uncle Tom himself is another character, a slave sold off to Simon Legree, a brutal and uncouth slave owner. So we follow two stories: the escape of the young slave girl to Canada, which is perilous, and her reunion with her husband—that's the happy story, although it's a terrifying one. We also follow the story of Uncle Tom, sold into horrendous conditions, to a fiendish man. He's finally beaten to death by his new owner, a genuine sadist. In the course of the novel, we learn a good deal about the institution of slavery, including how slaves are bartered and sold. We learn about what the slave master could do, if he chose, to a slave. We see from the very insides the working of this insidious institution, and its effects. In fact, W. E. B. Du Bois meditates on the effects of slavery in *The Souls of Black Folk*.

Tanenhaus: Which is another book you've included.
Parini: Yes. Du Bois, writing in 1903, looks back at the second half of the nineteenth century and said, "Okay, the slaves have been freed, but the wounds of slavery are deep, and how will we ever overcome them?"

Tanenhaus: He was a black author with a degree from Harvard?
Parini: The first black man to get a Ph.D. from Harvard. He was a brilliant fellow who grew up in western Massachusetts in the Berkshires, which was hardly a normal situation for a black man.

Tanenhaus: When was he born?
Parini: 1868, soon after the Civil War. So he grew up in the period after slavery.

Tanenhaus: He was really a social scientist, wasn't he?
Parini: After being a student of history, he became a kind of founding father of sociology.

Tanenhaus: What does he write about in *The Souls of Black Folk*?
Parini: There's a famous line that underscores the theme of these essays. He said, "The problem for the twentieth century is the color line."

Tanenhaus: So he means a problem not just for blacks.
Parini: For all Americans. He believed race would become the defining is-

sue of the twentieth century, not just in the United States but throughout the world. The wounds of slavery in this country are so deep, of course, that they're only beginning to heal. It's interesting to see a brilliant intellectual like Du Bois, early in the twentieth century, thinking about matters of race in such provocative terms, wondering about the position of black people in American society.

Tanenhaus: The book is written, as you say, in a very kind of exalted, quite literary prose.

Parini: Yes, and it's hard to imagine the audience for *The Souls of Black Folk*, although we know it went through edition after edition, and it has pretty much always been a touchstone for thinking about race in this country. Du Bois was speaking to a cultivated black audience, of course; but also to the liberal white intelligentsia, the people who might have the power to make changes in American society. The book was written in response to *Up from Slavery* by Booker T. Washington. I could have chosen these two books together. I do, in a sense, play them off each other.

Tanenhaus: In a way, they're a kind of yin and yang of the race issue.

Parini: They really are. For white people, Booker T. Washington was a huge figure. He argued that black folks, to use the term of Du Bois, should not worry about white society but create their own educational institutions; they should develop their own skills and get ahead in the world on their own, since the white folk were not going to help them very much. He essentially gives white people a pass.

Tanenhaus: And what argument does Du Bois make to counter Washington?

Parini: He argued that we should educate black people, "the talented tenth," as he called them. He wants to work with white society, if possible. To get their help. The importance of Du Bois is that he frames the racial argument in ways that continue to play out throughout the twentieth century. He implicates white people in ways that Booker T. Washington avoided, not wishing to cause trouble. Du Bois was combative.

Tanenhaus: Now, you discuss a third classic that deals with race: Mark Twain's great *Adventures of Huckleberry Finn*.

Parini: It's the story of a boy from nowhere—again, this harks back to Ben

Franklin—Huck Finn is an orphan boy, more or less. His father's a drunk who doesn't look after him. He has to make his own way in the world.

Tanenhaus: His father beats him.

Parini: Yes. So this boy—raised in Hannibal on the banks of the Mississippi—breaks away from civilized society. He's almost a black boy himself. One of the arguments somebody makes, and I talk about it in my book, is that Huck himself is nearly a black kid. He uses a lot of black dialect. He's certainly an outsider.

Tanenhaus: And his closest friend in the novel is a black man.

Parini: He's called "Nigger Jim." Huck Finn and Jim, this escaping slave, take to a raft, and they sail down the Mississippi toward freedom. One of the themes of *Huckleberry Finn* is lighting out for the territory. At the end, Huck votes in favor of liberating Jim. He's willing to break the law in order to support this black guy.

Tanenhaus: In fact, he thinks it's an immoral act to do it. One of the great passages.

Parini: Great passage! He says, "Oh my God. Do I dare break the law here, and not turn in this black slave to his rightful owner?" And he says, "I don't care. I will break the law." So civil disobedience, interestingly enough, comes into play here.

Tanenhaus: How popular was *Adventures of Huck Finn* when it was published? Twain was already America's most popular, beloved writer, author of *Tom Sawyer*. This is a somewhat different book. Huck Finn does appear in *Tom Sawyer*. Twain conceived his novel, I think we know, as a truly serious literary work. Was it received that way?

Parini: It was banned from many libraries. Some reviewers and librarians disliked the "rough" language in the book—Huck enjoyed his cussing. In the nineteenth century, because of the perceived indecency of the language, and in the twentieth century, because of its treatment of race, this became one of the most banned books on record. It still is.

Tanenhaus: Why would it be banned today?

Parini: The phrase "Nigger Jim" sounds racist. But you're a poor reader if you read this book and believe that Mark Twain was in any way a racist. If anything, this is a book about American freedom. It's about the possibilities of post-racialism. This is our primary American text, our greatest novel. It's a book I've reread throughout my life, and, a classic text. A classic is a book you can reread at different stages in your life; at every turn, it will inform your life in fresh ways.

Tanenhaus: Let's talk about a very different kind of classic that I was a little surprised to see on your list, but it's fun anyway. And that's Dale Carnegie's *How to Win Friends and Influence People.* When was that book written, and who was Dale Carnegie?

Parini: There are just two books of my thirteen that reviewers think are a little cuckoo. One is *How to Win Friends and Influence People.* The other would be Dr. Spock's *Book of Baby and Childcare.* But let's focus on Dale Carnegie. When I was a twelve- or thirteen-year old kid, I was shy, living in Scranton, Pennsylvania. I had few friends, and I didn't know how to talk to people. One day I was in a department store, and I saw this paperback called *How to Win Friends and Influence People,* and I thought, "That's for me." So I took it home, and I read through Carnegie's ways of making friends. He said, just to go with the first suggestion, "Find something to praise in everybody, as everybody's got something good about them. If you find that, and you focus on that trait, this person will be very happy. You'll be able to start a conversation."

Tanenhaus: So this is one of the great how-to and advice classics. Books like this come out all the time. What sets this one apart? It's still with us. Why?

Parini: There's a special tone. The book appeared in the midst of the Great Depression, when millions were out of work. People wanted to get control of their lives. And here was a way to manage that. Carnegie said, "You can take things into your own hands." In many ways, he's the twentieth-century version of Ben Franklin. There's a dark side to it, of course—a subtle recommendation that you ingratiate yourself with your boss. Getting ahead means putting yourself behind.

Tanenhaus: What was Carnegie's background?

Parini: He was a poor boy from the middle of nowhere from the Midwest who became a hugely good salesman. At one point he moved to New York City and took acting lessons, learned how to present himself. There was a lot of interest in sales in America, going back to Sears Roebuck catalog and before. Carnegie offered a plausible sales pitch, pulling together conventional wisdom on how to become an effective salesman with basic, admirable spiritual advice. I regard this book as a religious book, believe it or not.

Tanenhaus: How is it religious?
Parini: The core of every religion is the idea that you must lose yourself to find yourself. What matters is how we get along with other people. How we help other people and build community. Carnegie understood this. He quotes Christ. And the Buddha. He quotes various Oriental scriptures. This book is wise in unlikely ways.

Tanenhaus: Was he well read?
Parini: Well, he found good quotations. I doubt he was actually an intellectual, but there's a unique style in this book, which I still find riveting. I hadn't read it since I was thirteen. On rereading it, I found myself prickling all over. Here is the American character, undiluted.

Tanenhaus: Now, you also discuss a second advice and how-to book that has probably shaped a lot of us, even if we don't know it. And this is Benjamin Spock's classic *Book of Baby and Childcare*. What makes this special? There have been so many books on the subject. This one seems an enduring classic.
Parini: I'm a parent, and I've raised three children, with my wife. Beside the bed to this day is Spock's book. My parents used this guide. Spock was ingenious in speaking personally to the parent. I remember that when my first child was born, in 1982, someone gave me a copy of Spock—a common gift to a new parent. I read the first sentence: "You know more than you think you know." It was reassuring.

Tanenhaus: What did he mean by that?
Parini: That there is such a thing as the parental instinct. You must trust your own judgment. Spock invites us to use our rational faculties when we think about raising children. He's constantly saying, "Look, do the commonsensical thing." If a young child is about to play with an electrical cord that you know is dangerous, don't scream at the child but quietly remove the obstacle. Spock warns us against using shame. This was a primary tool for raising children before Dr. Spock.

Tanenhaus: Do we know what books before his on the subject were like?
Parini: There were a lot of prior handbooks on baby and childcare, going

back to the nineteenth century and before. In fact, one of the earliest guides was written by the English philosopher John Locke. Often these books were written by preachers. It's not for nothing that shame played a huge part in child-raising before Dr. Spock. He asked us to apply rationality to the project. And that's why, when the sixties came along, and students took to the streets against the Vietnam War in the streets . . .

Tanenhaus: He was blamed for it all!
Parini: Vice President Spiro T. Agnew came on television, and said, "It's all Dr. Spock's fault! He raised these kids. Their parents read Dr. Spock, and they were too lenient on their children, permissive. Look at the results!"

Tanenhaus: Who was Spock? How did he come to the views that he held? He'd been a physician himself—pediatrician?
Parini: He was an upper class WASP who grew up in New Haven, went to Yale, rowed on the famous Yale crew that won a gold medal in the Olympics. He was himself a tall and handsome hero. He went to medical school, studying at Yale, then Columbia. He became a pediatrician in New York, famous locally for his ability to communicate with parents. A publisher came along and said, "How about putting this all down in a book?"

Tanenhaus: Do we know what became of his own children?
Parini: It'd be interesting to see, wouldn't it? He himself became a wonderful man, I think, in his last decades. He was an early advocate of controlling nuclear bombs, a pacifist.

Tanenhaus: And much involved in the peace movement of the 1960s.
Parini: Yes, and he went to jail at one point with the historian Garry Wills, another peace activist. I end my chapter on Dr. Spock with a beautiful recollection by Wills, who was taken into prison with Spock for civil disobedience. And he said, "Here was a man of great nobility whose main concern when he got into prison was, 'How are you? Are you all right?'" I find Dr. Spock a worthy guru.

Tanenhaus: Let's talk about your title.
Parini: *Promised Land.* I found that these thirteen books all spoke to each other. The phrase "promised land" popped up again and again. It's a Biblical idea: Moses leading the Israelites through the wilderness and seeing the land of Canaan—a theme running through each chapter like a watermark.

Tanenhaus: Are there any books that almost made the list of thirteen?

Parini: I hated to leave out any number of books. It killed me not to write about *The Grapes of Wrath*, for instance. I've written a biography of Steinbeck, and I wanted to do that one. It was massively influential. But you can't do everything.

Tanenhaus: You wrote a biography of Robert Frost. There is no work of poetry in this selection.

Parini: Right. I would have chosen Walt Whitman's *Leaves of Grass* if I were writing a study of the greatest American works. Robert Frost's *North of Boston* might have been a good one to include, or Sylvia Plath's *Ariel*. So many books of poetry have shaped my own life. But this is not about the great books. This is about books that represent turning points in American culture, that shaped our mental landscape, and imprinted on us certain ideas and feelings that even if we haven't read the books, we still owe something to their influence. These books are in our D.N.A. We cannot escape Ben Franklin. We cannot escape *Huckleberry Finn*. We cannot escape *The Federalist Papers*. We're affected by these books every single day. If you live abroad a lot, as I've done—I've spent ten years of my life in Europe—you know the American character, because you see it juxtaposed against, say, the European character. You realize that Americans are scrappy. They're hopeful. They're querulous. They have a strong sense of independence. They're always lighting out for the territory. They're always hopeful. They believe the promised land lies just over that hill. In fact, we can see it in the distance. If we can only will ourselves toward it, we can possess that miraculous kingdom.

Interview with Jay Parini

Shelagh Shapiro / 2010

From Shelagh C. Shapiro on *Write the Book*: http://writethebook.podbean.com/2010/11/02/write-the-book-interview-117-11110-jay-parini/. Reprinted by permission.

Shapiro: I'm Shelagh Shapiro, and this is *Write the Book*, the show for writers and curious readers. It's Monday, November 1, 2010. Today you'll hear an interview with Vermont author Jay Parini, whose latest book is *The Passages of H.M.*, a novel of Herman Melville. Jay Parini is a poet, novelist, biographer, and scholar. Among his seven novels are *The Last Station*—the movie version of which features Christopher Plummer, Helen Mirren, and Paul Giamatti—*Benjamin's Crossing*, and *The Apprentice Lover*. He has written biographies of John Steinbeck, Robert Frost, and William Faulkner, as well as *The Promised Land: Thirteen Books That Changed America* and *The Art of Teaching*, which is based on his columns in the *Chronicle of Higher Education*. In addition to teaching at Middlebury College and writing, he has appeared frequently on various programs for NPR, C-SPAN, and CBS, and now he gets to add The Radiator to his CV. When I spoke to Jay Parini last Monday, I asked him if Herman Melville was an important influence in his writing life, and if Melville was one of his favorite writers.

Parini: I've been reading Melville for over forty years. I realized the other day as I was going for a walk that the very first article I ever published was a review of a scholarly book about Melville's book-length poem, *Clarel*.

Shapiro: Oh?

Parini: I published it in a small Scottish journal, probably in 1972 or 1973. So I was interested in Melville even in my early twenties. Melville's one of those authors people catch onto quite early. Everybody reads *Billy Budd*, or "Bartleby, the Scrivener," in high school—at least, they did so in my day. Yet I wouldn't say I was an obsessive Melvillean. I was more interested in Robert

Frost—and other poets. But when I decided to write this book, I dove right into the work again, read everything.

Shapiro: So it was his work that interested you the most, or did you know a lot about his life? He had a fascinating life.

Parini: *Typee* and *Omoo*—his first books—were recollections of things that happened to him out in the South Seas or Hawaii. I loved those books. I also knew *Redburn* well, an account of his journey to Liverpool and to London. He had a fascinating life and traveled around the world, had large adventures. I was fascinated by the idea that he was kidnapped by bisexual cannibals in the Marquesas. How many of us get kidnapped by bisexual cannibals?

Shapiro: And live to tell the tale.

Parini: It's rare, something extraordinary. I also knew that the last thirty years of his life were a bust: he practically stopped writing, except for occasional poems or bits and pieces. He wandered the streets of Manhattan like a ghost, wearing dark glasses, cape on, big hat, with his walking stick. I'd read his granddaughter's memoir, and she says he pushed his wife down the steps and drank too much and was an impossible man. The last decades of despair and non-productivity caught my attention. It intrigued me that this man with such robust energy and intelligence just dried up, then emerged with *Billy Budd* at the end—a classic tale, one of the masterworks of American literature. The complex trajectory of his writing life fascinated me. He lived in relative isolation in the last decades.

Shapiro: Although he was surrounded by the famous writers in the middle years. He knew Hawthorne, and he met Dickens. Or his wife did.

Parini: Only his wife met Dickens. But Melville was, in a sense, surrounded by writers in the Berkshires. That circle included any number of well-known figures—from Hawthorne to Oliver Wendell Holmes, Catharine Maria Sedgwick, and many others.

Shapiro: You allow two narrators to tell Melville's story: his wife, Lizzie, and then H.M. himself. He was known to his family as H.M. I wonder how you decided that these would be the perspectives through which the story would best be conveyed.

Parini: I thought back to *The Last Station*, my novel about Tolstoy and his circle. There, I had many of the diaries before me from people who knew

Tolstoy during the last year of his life. They gave me incredible points of entry into his way of life, his mind. With Melville, I didn't have as many viewpoints. The person who knew him best was probably Lizzie, his wife. When I began to poke around, I found out there was almost nothing about her—a handful of letters, and very little else. I knew the basic facts of her biography: she came from a wealthy Bostonian family. Her father, Judge Lemuel Shaw, had known the Melvilles forever. Shaw was Supreme Court Justice of the Commonwealth of Massachusetts. He had been the best friend of Herman's father, who died when Melville was just twelve. So I knew the family context, the associations, who she was in that sense, but very little about her personality. The letters reveal practically nothing. She was a blank canvas, a sketch pad, inviting me to invent this person who saw Melville on a daily basis for decades. I decided to tell the story of Melville's life in a third person narrative, but one very close to him. It's almost him talking. But I didn't want to impersonate Melville. That seemed presumptuous. And it would have been hard to get the voice right. Melville would have been a very circuitous, ornate speaker, and I didn't want to mess with that. I much preferred a third person viewpoint—a speaker who is really me, writing close to Melville's voice. A third person narrator can know things that only Melville can know. It's what you would call a third person, limited narration.

Shapiro: You did try to imbue his voice with some of what you picked up on in his journals and letters?
Parini: Yes, and to suggest what Melville might have sounded like.

Shapiro: In his head.
Parini: Exactly. Often I quoted directly from bits and pieces of Melville's writing. Sometimes I'm parodying, or writing around, things he said. If you know Melville's work, you'll see that my text is littered with his phrases.

Shapiro: And talking about inventing Lizzie, at one point in the novel, you say, "Truth requires a certain boldness of invention, a willingness to remake reality." And then also, on the next page, you had John Troy say, "Everyone knows that the truth can't be told, not in historical writing. You have to make it up, else nobody will believe you." So it sounds like you're talking to yourself a little bit there.
Parini: I am talking to myself in those passages. I've always believed that you have to make it up to make it believable. Reality is so bizarre, who can believe it? The things that actually happen, if you put them in a novel, people

would say, "That can't be so." You have to take things down a peg to make them believable, at least in a novel. Fiction provides a rich and productive soil, and truth grows there, leafing out. And Melville's life was so full of fantastic adventures. Who could believe that twenty naked seventeen-year old girls swarmed the ship when these sailors arrived in the Marquesas, leapt up on the deck, and had sex with the sailors? It's what actually happened. And he really did have astonishing encounters with people like Nathaniel Hawthorne.

Shapiro: It's quite a life. Now, I'm curious, as far as Lizzie's concerned, and going back to how you sort of had a blank canvas to work with, did you know, in fact, that perhaps there was tension between Melville's mother and Lizzie?

Parini: There was a lot of tension in the household because Herman was a mama's boy. Except for the time when he was at sea, he was rarely without his mother nearby. She lived with her son and daughter-in-law through much of her life, and she lived a long time. She actually ran the household, a domineering woman. I suspect Lizzie would have been—at least my Lizzie—very shy in her presence, less than willing to put herself forward, a bit cowed by the ferocious quality of Mother Melville.

Shapiro: There's this incredibly beautiful passage at the end of the book where his mother is being critical of Lizzie, and he becomes irritated with her. And then she dissolves into tears, and they have this hug. You wrote: "And then all of a sudden, they were mother and son again." And I felt sympathy for Maria in that moment for the first time in the book, because, you know, you do have your little boy all your life, and then all of a sudden, you have to change your whole way of behavior toward your child. I thought it was really well done.

Parini: The great thing about historical fiction is that nothing changes much over the decades. Human nature is a constant. People often ask me: "How do you know what families were like in 1840?" Families were not much different in 1640 or 1240 or 1940. You find the same kinds of jealousies and affections and interests. The same things would have been happening.

Shapiro: Right. I wonder if maybe this is a good time to ask you to read something.

Parini: Sure. So that your listeners can get a little sense of the book, let me read a tiny bit here, when we're traveling with Captain Pease on the *Acush-*

net, the ship that was the model for the *Pequod* in *Moby-Dick*. And Toby is Herman's great friend, okay? Toby Greene. They're sailing toward the South Seas on the *Acushnet*, and this terrible Captain Pease is very rude to the 'Gees, or the Portuguese, sailors on board.

"Toby had also come to dislike Captain Pease. 'A right fool, he is,' he would say, under his breath. He hoped that Herman would concur, but H.M. said nothing explicit about Pease, as it would never change anything and he felt uneasy about disparaging an officer. In any case, Pease paid no attention to H.M. or most of the crew. It was largely the 'Gees whom he abused in public, ridiculing their lack of English, their cowering posture, their failure to respond to his every command, however arbitrary. The men generally did not object when Pease persecuted these outsiders, who could hardly defend themselves. To many, the Azoreans were a subversive and possibly threatening clique. Why did they huddle on deck as they did, whispering in their strange tongue, snickering and winking? The songs they sang made little sense. Why could they not learn English as every other foreigner aboard the *Acushnet* had done?

"Stories about Pease, true and less true, began to circulate among the crew. His perfumed presence only added to the dark rumors, and his lack of sociability fueled the animosity that rose in flames around him, devouring his authority. Jack Hall—" He's one of the first mates on board this ship. "—was the main source of anti-Pease gossip, and ordinary seamen in any case tended to believe tales arising from an officer.

"'He is dangerously peculiar, I fear,' said Hall one day, abaft. He leaned nonchalantly against the coaming and smoked a fat cigar, addressing the third mate, Wilbur Mallon, a slight fellow from Nantucket, who stood at the helm and nodded.

"As ever, Hall's voice was a deep bell, and the remark drew affirming looks from a number of seamen.

"H.M. worried about this, as one did not say such things aboard ship without consequences. Mutiny took different forms, yet it was always a grave offense. Pease might be mad, even a little cruel, but he was no tyrant."

That gives you a sense of life aboard ship in the 1840s and '50s.

Shapiro: I was struck by the sort of list of captains that seemed to be incompetent, or mean, or just short diagnosable. Can you speak to that?
Parini: Melville took three or four major journeys, and in almost each case, the captain was either a drunk, or a paranoid, or a megalomaniac. These kinds of captains crop up repeatedly in his fiction. There were usually mod-

els behind each of these characters. I had fun portraying this array of mad captains, who ran the ships that Melville sailed on with gusto, or distaste, or mistrust of their crew. Valentine Pease was among my favorites: perhaps the model for Captain Ahab in *Moby-Dick*. Melville often drew on people he'd met in the course of his life and travels for characters in his fiction—all writers do. But he mixed and matched, transforming passing reality into something deeper, something mythic. That was the idea, in any case.

Shapiro: It was interesting to me that Melville was so capable of living that life, putting up with some of these personalities when he was a young man on his adventures, and yet when he was having a much more quiet and sort of maybe easier life at home, that's when he fell apart, and wasn't really capable of putting up with what life had brought him.

Parini: He lived an exciting, adrenaline-fueled life as a young man—four consecutive years at sea, and probably another year or more at sea in the mix, if you count his later journeying. In subsequent years, he usually traveled by himself. These were the times when he was most alive, most himself. He became the real Herman Melville, the figure in his mind. When he would retreat to the family, to his wife Lizzie and the dominance of his mother, he grew depressed, drank too much, and lost a grip on his experience. But of course those were the times when he was writing. He had a ferociously productive stretch of writing books for about eight or ten years. At home, he worked compulsively, writing most of his major works—*Typee, Omoo, Redburn, Moby-Dick, Pierre*—in a relatively short stretch of time. By 1863, when he moved to New York, he was washed out if not washed up.

Shapiro: That's when he's in his forties?

Parini: Yes, and he's pretty much finished as a novelist by then. Through family contacts, he gets a job as a customs inspector, wanders the docks of Lower Manhattan. Then he retires, continues to wander the streets of New York for some years. He doesn't die until 1891, by which time he has become a ghost of himself. The great author faded, certainly from the public eye. On the other hand, Melville never actually stopped writing. *Billy Budd* continued to occupy his mind till the end.

Shapiro: It was interesting that Hawthorne said to him not to struggle, but to work very hard on his writing of *Moby-Dick*.

Parini: Work very slowly and without ceasing. That was in 1850 and 1851.

Shapiro: It's interesting, because it's almost like the older man foresaw that this couldn't last forever.

Parini: He realized that Melville would burn himself out with that kind of productivity. We know quite a lot about Hawthorne and Melville because some of that correspondence, fortunately, survived. Also, we have the journals of Hawthorne, where he recorded impressions of Melville that are quite extraordinary. We also have some of Hawthorne's wife's letters. Those are mostly real letters that I quote in my novel. Sophia Peabody—the wife of Hawthorne—was an evocative writer.

Shapiro: She talks about how he's a very attractive man, with amazing eyes. Yet the other side is that it sounds like his hygiene was poor, and depending on how close you get to him, he's either a very attractive or unattractive person.

Parini: He struck many people as a homeless bum: thoroughly askew. He didn't keep his beard very well; his hair was long and wild, at times. He was an early beatnik or hippy. He drank a lot, too—and he smoked. So he had a kind of a raw, manly, unkempt quality. And this is in opposition to Hawthorne, who would have been extremely meticulous and maybe even . . . I wouldn't say perfumed, but he certainly would have been well groomed. Nevertheless, Melville was attractive, if you stood at a distance. He was wonderfully handsome. In photographs, he seems like a robust and handsome young man. Probably quite wild in manner and aspect. Yet he had a manic depressive tendency. When he was manic and in public, he was appealing. The depressive side overwhelmed him at home. I don't think he could have been easy to live with.

Shapiro: At one point in your novel, Lizzie says "Authors are often quite vain, I believe." I wondered where that line came from. Is that just something that you thought she would have been thinking, given the circumstances of her life?

Parini: Well, she grew up in an elite circle in Boston. Her father was a friend of Henry Wadsworth Longfellow, and many famous authors of the Boston group gathered in his parlor. And that was the most influential group of writers in the nineteenth century: Emerson and so forth. Lizzie had seen firsthand the vanity of authors. It's all true, as in the chapter where Dickens comes to America in January of 1842. Her father played a big role in Dickens's tour of Boston. Lizzie met Dickens in her father's judicial chambers, and he entranced her. Dickens was an incredibly self-possessed and vain young man, and he came—at least in her mind—to symbolize what an author might be like.

Shapiro: His following treated him like people treated the Beatles.

Parini: I don't think we can imagine an author today who would command the kind of rock-star treatment that Dickens had. He was Madonna and, you know, Bruce Springsteen rolled into one. Even that doesn't quite make it. People of all ages loved Dickens. In marrying Herman Melville, Lizzie hoped she was marrying another Dickens. It's worth recalling that this wasn't a complete illusion. Melville was a bestselling author when his first book had come out. He was famous not only in America, but abroad as well. I think he was much more famous in many ways in Britain than he was in America.

Shapiro: And he went back to Britain to try to drum up interest in future books.

Parini: He often tried to do that. He had considerable acclaim, a genuine readership; then it faded. The *coup de grace*, ironically, was his finest and most original book, *Moby-Dick*, published in 1851 to tremendous silence. It got a few reviews, mostly uncomprehending. Melville was disappointed that Hawthorne didn't take the trouble to write a review. It might have made a difference.

Shapiro: Didn't he dedicate the book to Hawthorne?

Parini: Yes, he did.

Shapiro: So would that have been inappropriate, to write a review of a book that had been dedicated to you?

Parini: Nowadays, you couldn't do it, but in the nineteenth century such a thing wasn't uncommon. Nobody thought that a review was necessarily objective. Not long after *Moby-Dick*, Melville published *Pierre*—just a year later, in fact. That book was considered really bad by most reviewers. One of the New York newspapers reviewed it with the headline, "Herman Melville Crazy." That suggests what they thought of him. After that, Melville withdrew, more or less, from public life. One little novel, *The Confidence Man*, and a bunch of stories, appeared; but that was it, really. Nothing else, except for a tiny volume of poems, self-published. Then came *Billy Budd*—a very late effort, unfinished at his death but certainly one of his most fetching and accomplished works.

Shapiro: I wanted to just back up a tiny bit. I mentioned the character John Troy, who was H.M.'s friend. You depict Melville as having fallen in love with Troy to some extent, although he felt conflicted about those feelings. I'm wondering, is this known to be the case, that he was bisexual, or at least in love with John Troy?

Parini: It's common knowledge that Melville had a strong homoerotic side to him. For instance, one of the first major biographies of Melville, published in 1949, was Newton Arvin's *Life of Melville*. He's pretty explicit there about it. He cites all of the homoerotic passages in the fiction. If you read carefully through *Typee*, *Omoo*, and on, you will notice this strain in his work. James Creech has written a whole book about Melville's homoeroticism. It's everywhere in the poetry and fiction that Melville wrote, from beginning to end. If you read the biographies, you can't help but notice he had endless attachments to younger men, such as Toby Greene. When he jumped ship in the South Seas and was captured by cannibals on the island, he had Greene with him, and he was very taken with Green. But we don't know whether there was any actual homosexual activity. There wasn't even a word for that, not in those days. I don't believe the word came into public view until much later, in the late Victorian period. I would be surprised if Melville had any sexual contact with men, although it wasn't uncommon on whaling ships.

Shapiro: You make it sound like John Troy, certainly in your vision of this experience, would have not been open to that.

Parini: I think not. Most of the men that Melville was attached to would not have been open to explicit sexual contact. So I would guess his feelings were repressed. In my book I never suggest that it's anything but a covert homoeroticism, a sublimated bisexuality, that occurs in Melville. He was certainly a practicing heterosexual, but a sublimated bisexual. This makes sense in reading his work. When you finally get to *Billy Budd*, you see this yearning for Billy and vivid descriptions of homoerotic feeling. Reading this short novel, it's hard to believe this wasn't a streak in Melville's psyche. He felt compelled to write about it—over and over. Scholars accept this as common knowledge, but I suspect it's news to casual readers.

Shapiro: Going back to Toby Greene: he disappeared, basically, on that cannibalistic island depicted in *Typee*. Was he ever seen again?

Parini: When *Typee* came out, reviewers suggested that Melville was just making this up. Well, Toby Greene stepped forward, saying "Here I am." He visited Melville in Albany. After he escaped from the cannibals, going to get help for Melville, he himself fell ill. He couldn't make it back to the island in time to rescue his friend. Communications were difficult in those days. You couldn't just send an email. Melville didn't have a Blackberry. What's fascinating is that Greene vouched for everything in *Typee*. Yet I still believe a lot of this novel is exaggerated or made up, a blend of fiction and nonfiction.

Shapiro: The way you organized the book, we meet the older, really flawed and troubled Melville early on, and then, as the plot unfolds, we get to know the younger, more carefree, curious adventurer—the younger man. Why did you let us see the older man first?

Parini: My hope was that it gives us a little bit of dramatic irony. Early on we learn that Melville, for example, didn't make any money as a writer, but then we can go to show him as a young man having this not untypical fantasy that he will make a lot of money as a writer. So when we see his failure, it's in an established context. That's dramatic irony, to a degree. I like being able to show us where Melville got to, to some degree, and then go back and visualize what he was like as a younger man. Then the narrative builds to the end, where we're back in real time again. Novels are, of course, time-traveling vehicles. You enter into warps or loops of time. A novelist shapes time, bends it. Life itself doesn't have that advantage, being strapped to dull chronology. So we're hopping around in time until the end, when we're suddenly in real time, or moving out of time.

Shapiro: I found it interesting, too. Because the first chapter is from Lizzie's perspective, and I enjoyed seeing how you envisioned their courtship and marriage, but getting there later was interesting. At the beginning, we see that there are problems in their marriage. It's a very troubled marriage.

Parini: You can see how it developed, this complicated but not unloving marriage. I hope readers will understand that it was quite a good marriage, in the sense they worked through their problems like adults. By the end it was very affectionate. I quote as one of my last epigraphs that memorable poem by W. H. Auden called "Herman Melville," which begins, "Toward the end he sailed into an extraordinary mildness." And there *was* that mildness at the end. He had come to terms with success and failure. He had rediscovered the fiction-maker in himself in *Billy Budd*, and he had found himself again in the marriage. It's a touching story, in a peculiar way.

Shapiro: He lived to what, about seventy?

Parini: Seventy-two. It was in middle age there that things went seriously awry, and that's when Lizzie tried to get her brothers to kidnap her.

Shapiro: Is that a true story?
Parini: Absolutely. She wrote to her brothers in Boston and said, "Please, find somebody in New York to kidnap me and take me back to Boston." And they wrote to say, "That's not possible. If you want to leave Herman, leave him." They were lawyers: "We'll arrange for a legal separation." She said, "Oh, that would be too embarrassing. I can't do it." And that's the last it ever came up. She decided to take the bit between her teeth and move forward.

Shapiro: Other than Melville—and I know that there have been many, because you write about them—can you talk about some of the writers who have influenced you?
Parini: I could mention Robert Frost, Gore Vidal, Steinbeck, William Faulkner, Walter Benjamin, Tolstoy. All the writers I've written about would be obvious ones to name but, in a sense, misleading. In my own life, possibly the most influential writer has been Alastair Reid, a Scottish poet and essayist who was my mentor in Scotland at the University of St. Andrews. We've remained friends through life, very close. Robert Penn Warren was another friend, a Vermont neighbor. I spent New Year's Eve with him and his family for many years, and we're all quite close. Reid and Warren probably influenced me more than any other writers. Quite early I met Seamus Heaney, and he had a strong influence on my poems. I've never lost touch with Seamus, although I see him too infrequently. A number of writers played a large role in my early days.

Shapiro: Did I hear correctly that Alastair Reid introduced you to Borges?
Parini: Jorge Luis Borges, yes. That was a memorable time in my life, over forty years ago. I had interesting conversations with Borges, and I've continued to read him carefully, to reread him. His understanding of time and fiction played into my early education. I reread his stories obsessively, and his poems as well.

Shapiro: And Pablo Neruda?
Parini: That's right. Alastair was translating both Borges and Neruda. They both came to Britain to meet Alastair, and through Alastair, I met both of these writers. I've loved Neruda's work ever since.

Shapiro: I think I heard you speak once about the experience of meeting Borges, and there was some interaction on the beach. Did you walk the beach with Borges?
Parini: Yes. I walked on the beach with Borges. He said he wanted to recite the Anglo-Saxon poem "The Seafarer" to the sea, and he spoke Anglo-Saxon.

Shapiro: Oh my.
Parini: He was blind, Borges. He let go of my hand. He started walking, racing toward the sea, and he got himself turned around. He was actually standing overlooking the golf course, reciting "The Seafarer." I was too embarrassed to say, "Borges, you're looking the wrong way." Borges and I, I took him out in a friend's car one afternoon. Alastair asked me to babysit Borges. We went driving off along the East Neuk of Five, and I said, "Mr. Borges, what would you like to do?" He said, "I'd like to go to a pub." I took him to a very basic Scottish pub, with sawdust on the floor, bare wooden tables. I didn't really know who Borges was, didn't realize he was one of the four or five greatest writers of the twentieth century. I said to him, "So, Mr. Borges . . . " He said, "Just call me Borges." "So, Borges," I said, "Alastair tells me you're a writer." He said, "Oooh, Alastair's always exaggerating." "So you're not really a writer?" I asked, dismissively. He said, "Oh, I've written these little stories and a few poems." I said, "Well, have you written novels?" He shook his head. I grew very contemptuous, "Then you've never written a novel?" "No." I said, "Well, did you ever want to write a novel, Borges?" He said, "Jay, my dear boy, my whole life I dreamt of writing the great novel of the Pampas in Argentina." And he said there would be gauchos, and there would be prostitutes, and there would be patricide and matricide and fratricide. Generations would rise and fall. Economies would boom and bust. He said, "Decades elapsed and I never wrote this novel." And then, after a dramatic pause, he added, "Then one morning, I woke up, and I went to my desk, and I wrote a brief review of this book. And that satisfied the impulse."

Shapiro: You read him now?
Parini: I reread him rather often. Likewise, Neruda was an amazing experience. Alastair took me to a reading Neruda was giving at the Royal Festival Hall in London. We had dinner with Neruda and went off to this reading. It was during all the troubles in Chile, and Neruda was the Chilean ambassador to Paris at the time. There was shouting and screaming from the audience. A riot broke out. In fact, in front of me, this guy was shouting horrible

things at Neruda, who was trying to read his poetry. A woman sitting next to me, a very perfumed, Latin American woman, took off one shoe, with a very sharp heel, and she brought it down with full force on the back of his head. He was a bald guy, and he bled like a stuck pig.

Shapiro: Oh my gosh . . .

Parini: The guards shrieked, and there was blood in the aisle. They pulled the guy kicking and screaming out of the auditorium. There was pandemonium in the place, with various Chilean factions shouting at each other. Suddenly Neruda went up to the microphone, really close, raised his hand like Moses parting the Red Sea, and he began chanting his great poem, "The Heights of Macchu Picchu" in a sonorous, deep voice. He quelled these waves of pandemonium. The room swelled with his poem.

Shapiro: As if he hypnotized everybody?

Parini: He hypnotized us all. Such a marvelous figure, one of the most impressive creatures I have ever encountered. Later I went to Neruda's houses in Chile. He had three idiosyncratic houses, and I went to all three of them, including this magical house at Isla Negra, which is about an hour and a half south of Santiago. He was dead by then, but I went to pay homage. And at each of these houses, above his desk was the same gigantic blowup of Walt Whitman, who was his hero, his muse. I've retained more than a passing interest both in Borges and Neruda my whole life. Alastair's translations of Neruda are, in my view, the most fetching.

Shapiro: I've heard that you enjoy writing in restaurants, and that in your life you've gone through phases where this was your habit. This is a paragraph that you wrote in your book *Some Necessary Angels: Essays on Writing and Politics*. You said, "Restaurants provide a kind of white noise, but—unlike real white noise—the sound is human. Noses are blown. People cough. You're reminded of the world of phlegm and digestion. And you feel connected. There is also a strange but unmistakable connection between cooking and writing—writing, like cooking, is a bringing together of elemental substances for transmutation over a hot flame. It seems fitting that writing and cooking should be going on simultaneously under the same roof." I enjoyed that.

Parini: Almost every morning I go to a café or a diner, and I work there at a quiet table. The bustle calms me. When I taught at Dartmouth, I often wrote in Lou's, a local diner. In Middlebury, I've tended to work in Steve's Diner or Carol's Hungry Mind Café. The latter has become a home away from home for me, and the owner—John Melanson—is a good friend. We often talk about literature, politics, the state of the world. A café is a lovely closed society, with a surprising intimacy. You meet your friends there, chat, trade stories, work, think. You cultivate leisure.

Shapiro: And don't you find that it's difficult to have people seeing you, recognizing you, coming over and saying, "Hey, how's it going?"
Parini: For the most part, people let me alone. But I'm sociable by disposition: my wife says I'm a thorough extrovert, which means I find it energizing to be with people. I don't mind seeing friends, talking. I will look for any excuse not to write.

Shapiro: At one point you write of Melville, "If he could not attend a school, he could read and reason. More important, he could write. He knew he could write, had always known this. It was his great and wonderful secret, a private stash of self-worth. He could put into words things unimaginable, except by himself." Just reading that, it struck me as a sort of universal experience for writers—young writers, in particular—that people who write discover early on that they enjoy doing this, and it's almost like a secret place they can go for comfort. I wonder if that's how it was for you.
Parini: That's exactly how it was for me, and I think that's probably so for you and every writer. You discover a place you can go—an interior realm. You find clarity there. Putting into words is the work of writing. It's exhilarating and reassuring. I don't mind my retreat into that world, where I find myself or, perhaps, make myself. It's the work of creation, and self-creation.

Shapiro: Have you ever had a period of time where it was difficult to go every morning?
Parini: Not really. I've had periods when I haven't written as much, for one reason or another. Usually family situations, or travel, or something unexpected intervenes and dislodges me from the routine I love. There are periods when I'm less energetic, perhaps, and then periods when I'm writing in a blaze and doing a tremendous amount—more than seems possible or healthy. Sometimes I write a tremendous amount of poetry, sometimes not. I go in and out of phases. Because I write in so many forms, there is usually something to attract my attention. I can always write a book review or essay, or turn my attention to editing. The Israeli writer Amos Oz is a friend of mine—I've been to Israel a couple of times to visit him, and he stayed with

me in Vermont not long ago. He once suggested to me that being a writer is like being a shopkeeper. You have a job. You go to the shop every morning, unlock the door, and stand behind the counter, hoping that customers will arrive. If nobody comes, you can dust the soup cans or wash the front windows. I spend a lot of time dusting the soup cans.

Shapiro: You've got to show up in case somebody does.
Parini: That's it. Often when I go to the café to write poetry, for example, I don't feel like it as I'm driving into town. But when I get there, sitting at my table, I find myself writing. I uncover a poem. That poem would never have existed had I not forced myself to sit there, pen in hand, notebook open to a blank page. I love that Woody Allen line: "Ninety percent of life is just showing up." Writers know that.

Shapiro: In doing a bit of research for this interview, I read Christopher Benfey's review of *The Passages of H.M.* that appeared online in the *New Republic*. A great review.
Parini: Yes, I liked it.

Shapiro: He writes, "Parini has written elsewhere of the necessary *mythos* of a successful biography, the narrative arc that compels our conviction in the unified meaning of a lived life." He goes on to say that your novel similarly used mythos in this way. So, in finishing this interview, I wonder if you can talk a little bit about this concept, and specifically about drawing on the story of Ulysses, which you did in creating the narrative arc.
Parini: *Mythos* is just a Greek word for "story," perhaps a story with metaphorical or symbolic resonance of some kind.

Shapiro: Right.
Parini: You have to find a shaping story—something that guides your writing, that draws the details in a certain direction, combs the material one way and not another way. Certainly, Melville was interested in Homer. He traveled with his copy of Chapman's translations in his suitcase. He was interested in *The Odyssey*, in particular. Being a seaman himself, a wandering sort of fellow, he identified with Odysseus. And, of course, Odysseus is the wandering hero hoping to get back to his wife, back to the marital bed that was made of oak and rooted in the earth. All romantic stories about the return to home. I think that to some degree, it's that oscillation between travel and returning that is always so important in Melville's life, and in the

work, as well. I think of Ishmael's wanderings. Tommo is the character in *Typee* who stands in for Melville, another wanderer. These people dream of going home one day, but they're adventurous, they want to push out, to put themselves at risk in some way. So the figure of Odysseus provided an organizing myth for my story. It's about setting out to wars, going into the world, having encounters, slaying the heads of beasts, and being captured. It's about confronting sexual beasts, philosophical and intellectual beasts, fighting with the critics. In this case, it was literal as well as figurative, the wandering. Melville did go everywhere on earth, around the globe many times. He went around the Horn, to the Pacific, to the Middle East—that was a moving journey for him—and everywhere in Europe. But he always returned to his mother, and to his wife. He ended right there in the marriage bed. So, in many ways, he's Odysseus.

Shapiro: This week's *Write the Book* prompt was suggested by my guest, Jay Parini. When I asked if he had any ideas for a prompt, his answer was so eloquent and swift, that I asked if I could air it in his own words. Here it is.
Parini: If you're writing a poem, for example, it's important to have one deep image at the center of that poem. Think of an image and try to reinforce it with concrete details. It works for prose as well, to begin with an image. See something. I always tell my students, in writing prose, if you're stuck, go through the senses: sight, smell, sound, taste, touch—the five senses. Try to make a gesture in the direction of each one of those senses. Describe a landscape, for instance. So I'm looking out the window. I see that the autumn light slants across the field. I smell the dry leaves with their musty damp. I hear the leaves rattling. There's a cool breeze playing cross my skin, which I can feel. I taste the slight acidity in the air.

And—boom—you've got a fall scene. So write for the senses and create images. Remember that an image is not just a picture but, as Ezra Pound said, it's a kind of psychological and emotional complex that moves in time.

Reflections on Biographical Fiction

Michael Lackey / 2012

From an interview on September 19, 2012, with Michael Lackey.

Lackey: Let me start by discussing one of the most important books written about the historical novel, Georg Lukacs's *The Historical Novel*, which was published in the late thirties. Most scholars consider it one of the most insightful and exhaustive studies of the historical novel. But there's something really troubling about the book, especially in relation to your work. He argues that the biographical form of the novel is doomed to failure because the focus on "the biography of the hero" leads authors to overlook or misrepresent significant historical events and truths, and thus "reveals the historical weakness of the biographical form of the novel." Given the nature of Lukacs's critique, he would say that your *Last Station, Benjamin's Crossing*, and *The Passages of H.M.* are not just failures—he would argue that they were doomed to failure from the outset because the very form of the biographical novel is limited and even flawed. How would you respond to Lukacs's critique?

Parini: First, let me say that I did read that book. I read it in 1968 or '69. So I read it a very long time ago, when I was at St. Andrews, in Scotland. It was a book that I happened to come across in the library. So I've in mind for quite a long time the idea that the biographical novel might be a flawed form, potentially lethal for a novelist! But I'd always been drawn to historical fiction and read a lot of historical fiction, admiring such books such as *Lotte in Weimar*, Thomas Mann's biographical novel. I was drawn to the idea of books centered on real historical figures. Having been a great reader of standard biographies, I realized at a certain point that it was simply all narrative, and that narrative is necessarily a form of fiction. In the course of time, I came to realize that Lukacs had it wrong; that, in fact, there's no appreciable difference between history and fiction in terms of narrative technique. It's all narration. Lukacs's argument, for me, didn't hold much water. It was flawed, in my view, because if you look at the examples of biographical fiction that we have before us in the last twenty years, we see again and again that the form can actually bring us closer to certain kinds of truths: truths unavailable in other genres. Biographical fiction shapes our ways of thinking about not only specific figures in a landscape, but it also takes us into that intellectual and cultural landscape and political landscape as well. It opens up our imaginations to a particular era. I've long believed that anything processed by memory is fiction. I don't know what kind of writing is not fiction, if truth be told.

Lackey: Let me ask a quick follow-up question. A number of people have referred to your novels like *The Last Station* as historical fiction. Do you think it's useful to call your novels historical fiction, or is there a benefit to actually saying these are biographical novels?
Parini: I don't think it's actually historical fiction, if only because that's a very specific genre that smacks of third-rate, dime store novels which give you a sweeping panorama with invented characters deposited in a fictional landscape. I'm doing something very different. And biographical novels are, too, when they focus and take as their main character, or at least as significant characters, actual people who lived in time, and open outward from that narrative, and while keeping to the agreed-upon-facts, nevertheless shine a flashlight into the darker corners of history and try to imagine what was really going on. So I think we're opening up perspectives here.

Lackey: So when you say "what was really going on," are you talking about the nature of human motivation? Are you talking about things that happened in the society that we don't really know about, that have not been recorded? What do you mean by that?
Parini: Just to play a little bit of a devil's advocate here: I recently read an interview with Bob Dylan where he says, "You can't do anything to change the present or the future, but the past is something you can change." I thought that was a crafty way of saying that we don't have any access to the future, and we barely have any purchase on the present. What we have is everything that happened behind us. So we're like the angel of history in Walter Benjamin: an image from a painting by Paul Klee. We turn our backs to the present and to the future, and we have the wreckage of history piling at our feet. In this wreckage, our job is to try and sort out something that fits into the category of "truth." That can be an emotional truth. It can be a factual truth. Obviously, in the biographical novel, we're not trying to excavate histori-

cal truth in the way professional historians are—although we sometimes do work with documents, interviews, and other materials that historians use. Nevertheless, we're trying to imagine truth. We're attempting to imagine ways of thinking about what might have happened, what could have happened. Rarely do we know what really happened. That's almost inaccessible. But at least we have the possibility of trying to imagine our way into the reality of something: Nietzsche's last night, or the reality of Tolstoy when he's dying in *The Last Station*, or the reality of Lincoln when he's dealing with the Civil War . . . We don't really know about the "truth" that lies behind such things. What can you do as a conventional historian with such events or situations? You can sift through limited documents, and you can quote those documents. But any time you begin to speculate on what those documents mean, you're moving into the area of imagining the past. So the biographical novelist simply gives himself or herself extra license and says, "I'm going to open this up. I'm going to let the floodlight of the imagination shimmer on what facts are there and try to see if there are pathways between those rocks."

Lackey: To make these abstractions more concrete, let's move to a specific example.
Parini: Good.

Lackey: In your novel *Benjamin's Crossing*, your Walter Benjamin believes that a Copernican revolution in thinking needs to occur. Here's how you describe the revolution: "Fiction would replace history, or become history." Can you clarify what this means? Would you say that we could use this idea in order to explain not only the rise, but also the value of the contemporary American biographical novel?
Parini: I agree with what Walter Benjamin says, that fiction ultimately should replace history. What I mean is that history should acknowledge its debt to fiction. History should understand that no matter how much it protests, it remains a form of fiction; that narrative involves the illumination of certain facts and the suppression of other facts. It has to do with the ordering of events. It has to do with trying to guess at motivation. And these are things that novelists do by trade. So ideally, the perfect historian of the future, if there's a new Copernican revolution, will acknowledge the fact that he's a fiction-maker, and that his work involves a grand ordering of events, the illumination and highlighting of certain things, and repression or suppression of other things. Shaping, in other words.

Lackey: A related question . . . Again, getting back to *Benjamin's Crossing*, can you briefly talk about the title of that work? How are you using the word "crossing" here? Specifically, how does the idea of crossing relate to Benjamin's experiences and philosophy?

Parini: Well, crossing means many things. On the most literal level, it's about Benjamin's crossing from France into Spain in 1940. There's a literal journey over the mountains. But it's really a symbolic phrase. It's about his transfiguration—his transformation—from, in some ways, a selfish, self-contained man who really had dismissed his own family, sent them off to England, and was living a life of narcissistic isolation, almost solipsism, working on his consummate project, a lost manuscript, in the national archives in Paris. History, in a sense—contemporary history—pried him loose from this cocoon and set him fleeing. In sending him afoot, he came into contact with Lisa Fittko, whom I interviewed at length, with Henny Gurlund, and José, her son. These were real people who crossed the mountains with Benjamin. So there was a figurative crossing of Benjamin from the narcissistic self-enclosed state he had been in for twenty years, sitting in the *Bibliothèque nationale*, to a much more humane person who was having to deal with the practical realities of getting over the mountain and dealing with his physical problems—he had a bad heart, for example—and the more spiritual realities of having to open himself up to these people, not only for his own sake, but for their sake as well, in order to get safely across the mountains into Spain. Ultimately, I believe he sacrificed himself so that they could proceed without him holding them back. It was almost a Christ-like act of self-sacrifice for the sake of other people, for their welfare. So this was a tremendous crossing for Benjamin—crossing in the sense of transfiguration. I think people are often transfigured. We don't know when or how or who. But I think there are transfigurations going on all the time. This is one of those crossings. I mean, the word "crossing" bears with it, of course, things like Charon's crossing of the River Styx in Greek mythology. I was thinking of all the different versions of crossing: from one state to another, from one mental state to another, from one literal place to another . . . It's a multivalent image.

Lackey: Can you talk just briefly about him crossing with regard to his identity? He was considered Jewish. Yet he would never really embrace it. Not because he didn't want to be Jewish—it was because he had a philosophy of crossing in the sense of ethnic crossing, moving from one kind of identity to the other. Did that play a role at all?

Parini: It did, in fact. I was thinking of this in a postmodern sense. Benjamin embraced so many different philosophies. He couldn't be pinned down. He couldn't be a Zionist. He couldn't be an Orthodox Jew. He couldn't even be a mystical Jew, even though he was very interested in moving toward Kabbalah and mysticism. I think he was in many ways an Emersonian figure in touch with the spirit, and he moved in ten directions at once. So his personality becomes extremely difficult to pin down or categorize. I think he, as a writer and intellectual, was an inveterate resister of categories. I mean, what was he? He wrote stories. He wrote fiction. He wrote book reviews. He wrote philosophy. He wrote art criticism. There was almost nothing he didn't try his hand at. His postmodernity involved shape-shifting, slithering among identities, taking on and jettisoning ideas with ease, a gleeful eagerness to resist being pinned down.

Lackey: Shifting to another topic here, you insist that your work is fiction; that it's not history or biography. This claim seems to establish a strict division between fiction and history, fiction and biography, as if fiction could not be used to shed significant light on a historical period or a biographical figure. Do you think it is possible for scholars like myself to use your work to shed new and important light on historical events and biographical figures? In other words, is it possible for biographical novelists to access a type of truth that traditional historians and biographers overlook? And if so, can you define the nature of that truth?

Parini: Well, I think you pointed out the fact that in each of these novels, I put up a warning sign saying "Don't be reading this as history, because it's fiction." That's my way of warning rather naïve readers not to imagine that they hold in their hands a work of history. If you bring those conventional expectations into play, you're in danger of possibly misreading the book that's before your eyes. But I'm speculating, again and again. In *Passages of H.M.*, for example: there was no way to know for sure the degree to which Herman Melville and Nathaniel Hawthorne were emotionally attached to each other—to what degree that relationship might have been homoeroticized. We can't know what happened behind closed doors. But I like to open those doors and try to imagine what could have happened. Again, the authors left traces, so one is not just grasping at straws. We have the journals of Hawthorne. We have Melville's letters to Hawthorne. So we have traces we can follow. But there is no clear path to truth. It stops well short of the door. The work of the fiction writer is to open closed doors and say, "Well, here's what might have happened on the other side of those doors." I think historians will have to become more comfortable with the fact that, whether they like it or not, they themselves are opening closed doors. The doors are there to be opened, and if they're not willing to step through them, they're limiting the possibilities of knowledge. What's the use of saying that there was this wonderful room, only the door was closed? You want to know what might be going on inside that room.

Lackey: But for the historians to make that move, wouldn't they have to first acknowledge that history is in some measure fiction? Once they make that concession, then they can see fiction as potentially getting to history. Is that right?

Parini: Yes. I think that the work of the historian would be amplified by the acquisition of skills that novelists have. One might ask for a greater use of the imagination and a freer use of the facts—I don't want to suggest that you should distort or misuse the facts—but I think you need to know what to make of the facts, and maybe allow yourself more room to play with them. It's a joyfulness of the imagination that I'm asking for, in myself and others.

Lackey: Shifting to a slightly different topic, one of the things I have noticed is that canonical scholars of intellectual and political history—and here I'm thinking about Erich Auerbach, Max Horkheimer, Theodor Adorno, Hannah Arendt, and Benedict Anderson—suggest that western culture has either been secularized or is in the grip of a rapid secularization process. But reading your novel *The Last Station*, it seems that religion and spirituality are very much alive. They may be changing form, but they are certainly not disappearing. Would you say that something in the nature of the biographical novel gives us a very different, indeed, a contradictory perspective about intellectual and political history from what we get in traditional scholarly studies?

Parini: Yes. Traditional scholarly studies tend to close out the spiritual aspect of human beings because that's not something you wander into easily, without personal, even moral, consequences. People tend not to be open about their spiritual lives. So it's difficult. Whenever you deal with an actual human being—we know this from everyday experience—there are layers and there are layers, and conventional historians often stick with, or get stuck with, a superficial layer. Many of the great intellectual historians that you've talked about—Adorno, Erich Auerbach—stick to historical surfaces, as if afraid to penetrate into the layers. I admire their work, of course; but I still would argue that they turn away from aspects of the subjects before them, bound by conventional approaches. I'm more interested in, say, the approach of Borges, who will take history and then turn it into fiction; turn it inside out and backwards. Borges is the great teacher, someone who understood how when he's writing a piece of literary criticism, it actually becomes a narrative, becomes a story. He starts imagining his way into the material, breaking through layers. In "Pierre Menard, Author of the Quixote" or "Tlön, Uqbar, Orbis Tertius," for example, you see him parodying conventional scholarship, upending conventional criticism and historical writing, showing his readers a literal mindedness at work in the academic world that is actually killing the truth. In order to find the truth, one has to imagine it. I've always loved that Oscar Wilde line that the English are "always degrading truths into facts." This is often true of literary critics and it's true of historians, intellectual historians especially. They're always degrading truths into facts. As a result, they often fail to arrive at spiritual truth. We now live in an incredibly religious age. If there's anything true about the modern world, it's this: religion is alive and well. People are trying to open doors to the spiritual life everywhere you look. The fact that modern secular history and historical science aren't willing to acknowledge this only shows that resistance is going to look more and more foolish as it completely contradicts the experience people have every day.

Lackey: Can you briefly discuss the narrative technique of your biographical novels? In all cases, there are multiple narrators, multiple perspectives. Why is this so crucial to your work as a biographical novelist? Also, can you explain how it is a logical development within the Western intellectual literary tradition? And finally, can you clarify how this technique sets the contemporary biographical novel apart from the traditional historical novel?

Parini: Well, traditional historical novelists, as in Sir Walter Scott, simply assume that history is verifiable and solid and ontologically stable, that a third person narrator can say, "In 1799, this army marched against that army," and believe they're getting somewhere near the truth. I suspect that the modern biographical novelist believes that truth is subjective and that every person's viewpoint is subjective and that truth is therefore idiosyncratic and resides in ways of framing the world and picturing it in language. People with their own linguistic gifts (or lack of them) have different degrees of access to interior realities. In my novels, I tend to layer subjective viewpoints. For example, in *The Last Station*, you're hearing from Tolstoy's wife. You're hearing from his doctor. You're hearing from one of his daughters. You're hearing from his publisher. You're hearing from his secretary. The narrative unfolds in five or six subjective viewpoints. You're hearing the same story

MICHAEL LACKEY / 2012 **119**

told from different angles of experience. By layering these viewpoints, there is a technique here for accessing truth. Now, what on earth would conventional historians have to do with any of this? They can't get at subjective truth. So, in many ways, a tremendous breakthrough in historical work has occurred. By analogy, this technique reaches back to the insights of Cubism. Picasso defined Cubism as a dance around the object. Whether the object is Tolstoy or Walter Benjamin or Herman Melville, I use these many voices to dance around this object, trying to open up the truth, looking for recesses where I can dig in and try to grow truth.

Lackey: This whole "question of truth" thing raises some serious questions about the responsibilities of the author and also the rights of the people who are the subjects of your novels. On your acknowledgments page of *Passages of H.M.*, you say that your book is a novel, not a literary biography. Even though your work is acknowledged to be fiction, is it possible that it infringes upon the rights of the subject under consideration? For instance, you say, "Very little is known about Lizzie Melville, so I made her up." Do you have any responsibility to Melville? An obligation to represent his life accurately? Can you specify the kind of liberties you feel justified in taking with the facts of Melville's life, and can you specify the kind of liberties that could not be justified?
Parini: That's a tricky but important question. If you look at the essay "Borges and Myself" by Jorge Luis Borges, he talks about how there's this fictional character Jorge Luis Borges who in many ways stands apart from the real self, who is Borges. These are different people. There will be a Jay Parini who exists in the public world and has a life apart from me. I think whenever you start launching representations of yourself into the world via letters or short stories or poems or novels or whatever, you sign on the dotted line a contract with the future. And in this contract, you say, "Okay, I have launched forth a character with a name similar to my own. I acknowledge therefore that this person—this projection—can be open to interpretations, and that the people in the future, posterity, will have the privilege of interrogating that projection and coming to terms with it." So we come to terms with a figure called James Joyce. We know some dark things about that figure. We know that he had a scatological obsession with his wife's underwear, for example. We know all kinds of horrible things about all kinds of people, from Napoleon through Hitler or Franklin Roosevelt or John Kennedy. Some of these things will be true, some will be exaggerated, some will be distorted . . . But again, we don't know anything really about Franklin Roosevelt, for

instance. What we know are something about the traces he left behind and some of the projections that people had in their own heads about "Who was Franklin Roosevelt?" I think one could do a weird, wacky, surreal novel in which Franklin Roosevelt spends much of his time flying in air balloons over France, and I think that would be within the boundaries of a surreal novelist. If he or she thought that that would get us closer to some aspect of the personality of F.D.R., let him fly air balloons over France for thirty years. He can live in that air balloon over France and call himself Franklin Roosevelt. He can spout ideas about the New Deal while flying over the fields of Provence. I don't see that anybody should worry about that. I doubt that Franklin Roosevelt himself, the actual man, would have cared. Roosevelt signed the deal that I've signed, allowing people of the future to project out this name and attach certain language to it. Posterity has the rights and privileges accorded to all imaginative creatures, which means they can play around with public material. They can move it around, rearrange the elements in ways that might have a clarifying effect. If people do this in an immoral or irresponsible way, that will show up. I hope so. To be frank: I felt a little guilty, for example, prying into the homoerotic impulses of Herman Melville. But I felt less guilty about it only because he opened himself up to this kind of inquiry in his own fiction. I mean, there's homoeroticism in everything from *Typee* through *Moby-Dick*, and of course . . .

Lackey: *Billy Budd.*

Parini: Exactly! The homoeroticism in this work is pervasive. So Melville—probably without being conscious of this—invited posterity to play around with that aspect of his soul. I thought I was fairly discreet on this matter. I didn't actually have Melville engage in any homosexual acts in my novel. I simply had him entertaining mild homoerotic fantasies and walking close to the line but never crossing it. My guess is—and that's, again, the hunch of the historian/fiction writer—that what I imagined might actually be true. I assumed I could get beneath his fictional world by probing into an imagined sexuality. So I think there are places that it would be immoral to go, but I think those lines, if they're crossed, become pretty bloody obvious to people, to readers. People will say, "You can't do that. That's just crazy." I think readers understand that when you're reading a work of history or a work of fiction, you need to trust the integrity of the writer, his or her fidelity to experience of the kind under examination, subjected to representation.

Lackey: All right, I want to shift gears at this moment. One of the virtues of interviewing you is that you have a commanding grasp of literary history, so you can talk about the evolution of certain aesthetic forms. And in this case, I want you to briefly talk about the way the historical novel has morphed into the biographical novel in recent years. Here's what I'm thinking. You were friends with Robert Penn Warren and Gore Vidal. *All the King's Men* is a traditional historical novel in that is based on Huey Long but it changes his name to Willie Stark in order to give Warren considerable freedom to alter historical facts. Vidal's *Lincoln* is different in that it retains the names of the original figures. Can you locate your work within this genre of writing, and can you explain why this particular genre has become so popular in the last twenty-five years?

Parini: This is a fairly recent phenomenon, for the most part. I mean, there are isolated examples going back to the eighteenth century. It's not as though it was invented from whole cloth. In various European languages, early versions of this kind of writing occurred. Thomas Mann, for example, played around with biographical fiction in fascinating ways. Some of the African American writers of the Harlem Renaissance toyed with it. In *All the King's Men*, written in the mid-forties, Warren felt tightly bound to the traditions of conventional historical fiction. I don't think he could see his way toward the contemporary forms of the biographical novel, or else he would have called his protagonist Huey Long, not Willie Stark. I wish he had. I think he could have written a better novel if he'd actually dug into Long, because I know he was obsessed with him. I had detailed conversations with him about Long. I recall sitting at the dining room table with Warren and Cleanth Brooks, his old friend, and they spent a whole evening telling wild stories about when they were at L.S.U. and editing the *Southern Review* and things that Huey Long said, did, and so forth. In many ways, those stories were wilder and more interesting than anything in *All the King's Men*. So I think Warren drew on the energies of the modern biographical novel without quite understanding what he was doing and where he was going. Warren's thinking and writing—his example—shaped my thinking at a very early stage. He was in many ways the most gifted and influential figure in my life. But when I began working on *The Last Station*, my first biographical novel, I was lucky to be living in Amalfi, in southern Italy, and my next door neighbor and close friend was Gore Vidal. He had just published *Lincoln* in 1984. Soon after this, I spent long evenings over glasses of wine talking with Gore about the nature of the biographical novel. And he kept saying to me, "We've got to put historical figures up front and center in our novels and use all the techniques and tools of the conventional historian, and yet bring to bear on this material the imagination that a good novelist has." And so I talked through the writing of *The Last Station* with Gore at every stage of its composition. He read it in rough draft form, several times. I think he really pioneered the genre with *Burr* and *Lincoln*. He found ways of putting front and center a real character. Of course he'd read conventional historians carefully. He really understood everything about Lincoln and his era. Gore was a real historian at heart. And he was a true novelist and creative artist. So he was able to illumine Abraham Lincoln in a way that his version of Lincoln will stand beside a dozen other Lincolns. The truth will reside somewhere amid all of them. Gore would be the first to say, "I cast up on a screen one version of Lincoln. Somebody else will cast up on that screen another version of Lincoln. And when you get the accumulation of all these different Lincolns, eventually people in the future will have a sense of this man: his motives, his triumphs, his failures, his difficulties." Novelists sensed an opening that postmodern theory created, and they have rushed into that space.

Lackey: Actually, that's my next question. What role do you think postmodern theory has played in the formation of the biographical novel? Here, I'm thinking about the way the postmodernists claim that truth is more a fictional construct than an ontological reality. How has this idea inflected our understanding of biography and history? And is there a logical connection between the ascendancy of postmodernism and the rise of the contemporary biographical novel?

Parini: I would guess that the rise of the biographical novel and the rise of postmodernism, with postmodern theories of truth, are directly linked. We couldn't possibly have the biographical novel in its current form if it weren't for the fact that truth has been—not so much deconstructed as reconstructed. That's to say, we now understand that truth is situational and that perspective plays a huge role in how we view anything. It's the old idea that if you look at the sedimentation in a rift in Africa, one person sees a certain kind of rock. Another person sees snails. It depends on what you're looking for. If you're coming at something from, say, a Christian perspective, you're going to observe patterns of self-sacrifice and bearing the cross and transfiguration. If you're looking at it from a secular viewpoint (or a purely capitalist or Marxist viewpoint), you're going to see a very different kind of pattern. You'll look for economic motives, for example. The fact is, every person brings an idiosyncratic lens to the camera and looks at reality through that lens and views different colors and different objects. So the same historical object will appear different to different people coming with different perspectives. So if you apply a Marxist approach, you're going to see certain things in history. If you apply a religious approach, other things. If you apply any one of a thousand different viewpoints, you're going to get a thousand different versions of reality. I think that the postmodern insight is that truth is not some hard, objective thing; it's an accumulation of subjective viewpoints. Truth is, in fact, constructed very carefully, although often unconsciously, because everybody is a gigantic prejudice-making machine. We all generate ideological formations that color everything we see. So it's almost impossible for two or three people to see the same thing and describe it in exactly the same way. The biographical novel affords an amazing possibility for the future, a way to translate history into a kind of truth that has been unavailable until this time.

Lackey: When you think about biographical novels—other people working in the genre—has anybody done something you'd say, "That narrative technique . . . Wow. That opens up things in a way that I had not seen before"; something that could be used in a new way to expand the borders of knowledge through fiction? Has anybody done anything that really jumps out at you?

Parini: I think Peter Ackroyd in England has done some astounding work, both as a biographer and as a biographical novelist. When he wrote his novel *Chatterton*—he did that maybe thirty years ago—he examined the life of the Romantic poet Chatterton in very interesting ways. Julian Barnes in *Flaubert's Parrot* was, I think, exploring biographical fiction in a unique and interesting fashion, too, opening up the life of Flaubert in ways that had never been done before. When Ackroyd in the early eighties wrote his massive biography of Charles Dickens, he included a number of fictional dialogues between himself and Dickens. To me, these innovations illumined and shaped the biographical passages written in a more conventional vein which preceded and followed it. So I think that some of these English writers, especially Peter Ackroyd and Julian Barnes, have been pioneers. In *Libra*, Don DeLillo showed how the biographical novel can add immensely to our understanding of key historical events such as the assassination of J.F.K. The main thing I came away with after reading DeLillo was the thought that the Warren Commission counts among the great fictional works of all time. I think we're going to see this happen eventually with 9/11. I mean, what's desperately needed for 9/11 is the imagination of history. Someone has got to go into that sequence of events from unique angles, perhaps try to get into the mind of Mohammed Atta, the Egyptian who flew one of the planes into the World Trade Center. A good writer has to grapple with the historically complicated, endlessly fascinating, tragic realities associated with 9/11, a multidimensional event that will never be fully understood.

Lackey: To bring this interview to a close, let me ask one last question.
Parini: Sure.

Lackey: What project is next, and how will it be a logical extension of what you have already done, and how will it chart new ground for you?
Parini: Well, the main book I'm working on—slowly, doing the research—is called *FDR*. It's a very long novel in which one takes this projection, the initials of Franklin Delano Roosevelt, in bright letters and throws them up into the sky like in Hollywood with those search lights that flash in the sky at night when there's a premier of a film. From 1920 up until 1944, the world, especially the United States, was utterly in the spell of this incredible creature who became a kind of blank screen on which countless ordinary citizens projected their ideas. I think that F.D.R. was a genius, in his odd way. He was able to re-create American politics. We've not yet come to terms with the full range of his genius, not even begun to explore the wild, almost Dionysian aspects of his life. His sexual energies were productive and strange and complicated. His own wife's homosexuality—her lesbian life—needs a good deal of sensitive exploration, as it played into her husband's sexuality, affected his politics. The open-mindedness that F.D.R. showed on this topic and so many other topics remains of huge interest to me. I'm hoping that in moving from literary figures to a political figure like F.D.R. I can extend the range of the biographical novel as I conceive of the genre. I want to use all the techniques of the conventional historian and the novelist in ways that hover on the edge of a new kind of history. That's my hope—maybe a fantasy. I don't know whether I will succeed. I've always believed in aiming high, even if I miss.

Lackey: Jay, thank you so much for sharing your thoughts with me.
Parini: It was good to think about these things. As I've always said, the biographical novel is one of the least theorized places in literary culture. It's time this were remedied.

The Uses of History in the Biographical Novel: A Conversation with Jay Parini, Bruce Duffy, and Lance Olsen

Michael Lackey / 2012

From a round-table conversation moderated by Michael Lackey at the University of Minnesota's Institute for Advanced Study (September 20, 2012): http://ias.umn.edu/2012/09/20/duffy-parini-olsen-biographies/. Reprinted by permission.

Lackey: Let me briefly start by telling you what led to this round-table conversation. Over the last couple years, I have read a number of biographical novels. What struck me is that there's virtually nothing written about this genre of fiction. I started to ask the question: why is this the case? One of the reasons—and I think there are many others—is that in the late thirties Georg Lukacs wrote an influential book called *The Historical Novel*. In that book, he makes the argument that the biographical form of the novel is a serious distortion of historical fiction and that it's actually something that should not be done. In essence, the biographical novel is by its very nature a flawed form. One of his arguments goes like this: the biographical novel could never rise to the level of a legitimate historical novel because the focus on "the biography of the hero" leads authors to overlook or misrepresent significant historical events and truths and thus "reveals the historical weakness of the biographical form of the novel." Most writers accepted this view. So before the 1970s, there were very few biographical novels. Three that immediately come to mind are Arna Bontemps's *Black Thunder*, which was done in 1936, Zora Neale Hurston's *Moses, Man of the Mountain*, which was published in 1939, and William Styron's *The Confessions of Nat Turner*, which came out in 1967. But starting in the 1980s, there was a veritable explosion of such novels. Let me mention just a few: Ron Hansen's *The Assassination of Jesse James by the Coward Robert Ford*, Gore Vidal's *Lincoln*, Bruce Duffy's *The World as I Found It*, Jay Parini's *The Last Station*, Irvin Yalom's *When Nietzsche Wept*, Parini's *Benjamin's Crossing*, David Mamet's *The Old Religion*, Anita Diamant's *The Red Tent*, Michael Cunningham's *The Hours*, Russell Banks's *Cloudsplitter*, Hansen's *Hitler's Niece*, Yalom's *The Schopenhauer Cure*, Lance Olsen's *Nietzsche's Kisses*, Edmund White's *Hotel de Dream*, Sherry Jones's *The Jewel of the Medina*, Olsen's *Head in Flames*, Parini's *The Passages of H.M.*, and Duffy's *Disaster Was My God*. There are many more. But how do we explain the proliferation of these novels? Why did so many writers disregard Lukacs's prohibition against the biographical novel? What changed in intellectual and political history that allowed these writers to write this kind of fiction? I contacted Jay, Bruce, and Lance in order to get some answers, and today I'm hoping that they will share some of their thoughts with us. Let me start by asking you three to define your novels. Would you call them biographical novels which also focus on history? Or, would you say that they are actually historical novels which just happen to use the life of a famous figure to illuminate a specific time in history? Or, would you agree with Lukacs and say that they focus almost exclusively on the biography of a specific person and, as such, are not terribly interested in history? Or, would you call them something entirely different?

Duffy: You first, Jay.

Parini: I go first? Oh dear. Well, I would say to hell with Lukacs. [Laughter] I did read that book when it came out. I was a graduate student at St. Andrews, in Scotland, where Lukacs was in vogue. When I got to writing *The Last Station* in the middle of the late eighties, I don't think I actually thought about his book or its argument. I tried to imagine what kind of piece of fiction I wanted to write. I didn't actually try to define it—not in theoretical terms—as I was writing *The Last Station*. I had become obsessed with Leo Tolstoy, and I wanted to look at his world really closely. I always believed that history is just a narrative. One of the greatest forms of fiction is called "history." History is fiction. As soon as we get into the business of putting reality into words, we're in the fictive realm. "Fictio" means shaping, and there's no such thing as an objective historian. I really believe that. Objective history is a piece of nonsense. Historians have tried to put one over on us over many centuries, going back to Thucydides. I'm more with Herodotus, who combined myth with history and understood that he was involved in a fictive enterprise. So when I write, I don't actually categorize my work. Yet I'm comfortable with the phrase "biographical novel" because three of the novels I've written are, in a sense, biographical. Most novels are auto-biographical, and the truth is most biographies are forms of autobiography. [Laughter] So really, it gets confused very quickly. I simply would be more comfortable saying I'm writing a narrative. My narratives sometimes involve real people. I'm projecting on the screen, creating characters and trying to imagine what they're really like. I hope I'm getting closer and closer to the truth as I write about Tolstoy, as I write about Walter Benjamin, as I write about Herman Melville. I'm of course looking for gaps where I can fill things in, but trying to imagine the past involves a huge effort of fiction—deploying the techniques of fiction. In short: as soon as we begin putting things into words, we're involved in the action of fiction making. I think if we're going to write a history of the Peloponnesian War or a history of World War I or a life of Franklin Roosevelt—as a straight biography—or an imagined life of Leo Tolstoy, we're on some level engaging in the same work, which is putting into words. And as soon as we begin putting things into words, anything that's processed by memory becomes fiction. I'm in the business of processing memory. It might be my own memory or it might be a larger memory. How's that for a start?

Lackey: That's a good start. Bruce?

Duffy: I've always resisted titles for fiction—the "Coming of Age Novel," for example. That said, "the biographical novel" is probably a title that has some practical staying power. If I got to choose, I would probably prefer something in the realm of "the novel of life and ideas" because that, I think, is what I write—and what we all write—really, books about ideas. As far as history and Lukacs, he is really coming out of a deeply Marxist perspective, so it's a—to my mind—authoritarian, top-down sort of view of history, very deterministic, and trying to control things. Not me. I think writing a novel is not about control. Quite the contrary. For me, the novel is about letting yourself be uncontrolled, letting yourself be really open and driven by other events, really, being confused. Actively finding confusion rather than trying to find certainties, starting off with some laundry list of what you think a novel should be. That, to me, is—sorry—disgusting. I think such control has nothing to do with fiction. I don't think any writer would ever think in this way. Honestly, I don't think it would be productive to produce a novel in this way, snapping together the puzzle pieces to reproduce some more or less accepted picture of history.

Olsen: What a pleasure to be invited to this party. And I'd like to preface my comments by invoking a famous/infamous essay by Wimsatt and Beardsley, "The Intentional Fallacy," which argues against the notion that authors know precisely what they're doing and that they can articulate their aims any better than any other practiced reader. I want to pair that essay with Roland Barthes's "The Death of the Author," which houses a kissing cousin of that idea, and suggest the guy who wrote *Nietzsche's Kisses* has very little to do with the guy mouthing these words today. I have a hard time remembering exactly what I meant to do [Laughs] when I was doing it. So I think the phrase that I would use to typify the sort of stuff we're talking about is "thought experiments in not-knowing." That is to say—okay, and now I'm going to digress, and I'll be back in just a second—that there is a basic lesson that the science fiction genre teaches us. What we think it teaches us is how to contemplate tomorrow. What it really teaches us is how we'll never know what tomorrow will be like. In an important way, that is, every science fiction novel gets it wrong. Okay, back to your question, then: it seems to me that so-called "biographical fiction" and so-called "historical fiction" actually teach us the same lesson about pastness and about identity, which is to say they're lessons in how we'll never know those beasts.

Lackey: Okay, let's move to another question. Consistent among you three is the tendency to alter historical fact. But is this legitimate? Is it fair to history or to historical figures represented in your work? For example, in *The World as I Found It*, a novel about the life of the philosopher Ludwig Wittgenstein, Bruce eliminates one of Wittgenstein's sisters from the narrative. Since Wittgenstein family dynamics play such a crucial role in shaping the philosopher's life, how can you justify eliminating this character? In *The Last Station*, a novel of Tolstoy's final year, Jay creates a lover, Masha, for Tolstoy's secretary Valentin Bulgakov. We know that Bulgakov had a lover, but we know nothing about her—not even her name. On what basis can you justify creating this character? And in *Nietzsche's Kisses*, Lance has Nietzsche's sister Elizabeth fire Peter Gast, who was a Jew and one of the first editors of Nietzsche's work. Historically, Elizabeth did fire Gast—but then she rehired him, which you do not mention in the novel, and eventually came to like him, something that you also do not mention. [Laughter] How can you justify your alterations of the historical record? Bruce?

Duffy: Do you really care that Wittgenstein had thirteen siblings as opposed to six? I'm being provocative. [Laughter] But the point is this: that from a dramatic point of view, from a narrative point of view, I wanted to try to tighten the lens on this family, so we know a few of them very, very well. I didn't think I could do this sort of Ringling Brothers thing with the thirteen siblings in the family and have a book that would be very interesting or intelligible. But more to the point, what I tried to speak to was the reality, the inner weather of Wittgenstein's life as a path to the deeper, more important reality of Wittgenstein's thinking. The work, the destruction and bravery of great thinking—that's what was important to me. Being a novelist, you are making choices, and you have to figure out—especially doing biographical novels—what you're going to stick to, dividing what's really important from what's not so important.

Parini: It's a very creepy question in some ways. [Laughter] "Don't you dare to alter the past!" When I was flying out here yesterday, I was in the airport in Burlington, Vermont, and I picked up *Rolling Stone* because my hero, Bob Dylan, was on the cover. And I said, "Well, an interview with Bob Dylan. Yet another one. I'm going to read it." There was something he said that was utterly, devastatingly true to me. He said, "Look, we can't change the present. And we can't change the future. But we can change the past." [Laughter]

Duffy: I like that.

Parini: And I thought, that's what I'm in the business of doing: I'm in the business of changing the past. It's our duty to change the past; we do it for ourselves all the time. For instance, I just recently finished thirteen years of psychoanalysis. I have completely changed my own past to suit my present psychological state. [Laughter] So as a novelist, I'm really in the hard work of changing the past—of altering reality—so that it can make sense to me and maybe make sense to some other readers. Lance? [Laughter]

Duffy: That's a provocative answer. I like that.

Olsen: Robert Browning once gave a poetry reading, or at least that's how our narrativization of the past goes. Afterwards, during the Q and A, someone asked: "Mr. Browning, what did you mean by that poem?" He said: "At the time I wrote that, only God and I knew what I meant. And now only God knows." [Laughter] That's sort of how I feel when asked questions like this. To harmonize with what you guys are saying: I believe there's an aesthetic logic that guides narrativity. Imagine trying to tell a story about Nietzsche or Wittgenstein or Tolstoy and not leave anything out, not shape it. That story would be tens of thousands—hundreds of thousands—pages long, and we would all stop reading pretty fast. I also want to frame my answer—and this goes to my earlier point about these kinds of narratives—by reminding us of Linda Hutcheon's notion of historiographic metafiction. She's talking about fiction that is highly aware of talking about pastness, we are always-already being written, rewritten, erased, reformatted and retold, edited. Her argument is—and I think it's an important one—that really these kinds of novels aren't about the past, but about the problematization of historical knowledge. Renarrativizing history points to history as a problem that writers are investigating. She makes an interesting distinction—I think it's one that we all sort of unconsciously as writers make—between facts and events. She defines facts as discourse defined, events as non–discourse defined. That is to say—and this goes back to what you guys are saying—as soon as you begin to tell a story, you move it from the real world into language. As soon as you move into language, you move into narrativity. As soon as you move into narrativity, you are talking about how you constellate facts around events. One can imagine, the Germans having won World War II, that the history of World War II would have been a quite different history than we now tell. All of which is to say: I left out what I needed to for aesthetic, but also, I think, epistemological reasons.

Lackey: In your novels, all three of you focus on figures who are deeply concerned with the condition of knowledge and formulate theories about knowledge. Lance, you focus on Nietzsche, specifically the role a will to power plays in the formation of a knowledge system. Bruce, you focus on Ludwig Wittgenstein, specifically how he initially rejected the role the Freudian subconscious played in the formation of knowledge but how he eventually came to understand and accept the power of the subconscious. And Jay, you focus on Walter Benjamin, specifically his rejection of metaphysical knowledge in favor of a de-essentialized, provisional form of fragmented and sometimes contradictory knowledge. Can you all briefly discuss what motivated you to focus on your particular writers, and specifically their theories of knowledge?

Olsen: My sense is that all theory, which is to say, all writing, is a form of spiritual autobiography. It has much less to do with the subject at hand than with the experience of the subject at hand filtered through a particular consciousness in the world. Or as J. M. Coetzee said: "All autobiography is autré-biography." As soon as you begin to talk about autobiography, you're narrativizing someone else. To your question, then. I want to say two events motivated me. One is that I spent the first few years of my life growing up in Venezuela. My dad was involved in setting up oil refineries. We lived in a jungle compound. It was just at that age when you're commencing to come to consciousness. I have a sister who was with me during that time, and, years later, as I was sitting with her, talking about these crazy events I re-member experiencing—snakes in the washing machine kind of events, be-ing chased through the jungle by a wild boar kind of events—I realized my sister was continuously getting it wrong. [Laughter] I was the only one who really remembered what had happened. [Laughter] That was fascinating to me—the slow understanding that we allegedly had these same experiences, but neither of us actually agreed on what the experiences were we had. We each narrativized them weirdly differently—to the point where stuff that my sister says happened to her, I vividly remember happening to me, and vice versa. The other thing that influenced me—well, you meet Nietzsche and, as Yeats says, you instantly become drunk on him. I did that as an under-graduate. I remember taking a course on existentialism and Nietzsche was on the syllabus, and, of course, to begin to read him is to never stop reading him. Also, to begin to read biographies of Nietzsche is immediately to real-ize how narrativized he is, how many versions of him exist in the universe. There's an existentialist Nietzsche, for example, a poststructuralist one, a crazy-man, a misogynist, a visionary, and so on. That intrigued me. Shortly after I graduated—in the late seventies, I think—maybe the early eighties— I wrote a story about Nietzsche, trying to capture the uncapturable, then thought I put him away. Maybe in 2001 I was walking by a bookshelf in my house and saw this line of Nietzsche books and thought, "I wonder if that guy still holds up?" [Laughter] I reached for . . . I think it was *Twilight of the Idols*, and started thumbing through it. Oh my God. I realized he had never left me. A way to deal with that unshakability turned out to be trying to write through his work.

Duffy: At some point, most novelists have a very humbling event—maybe several humbling events—and that is when a novel fails. You're writing a novel. You're spending a great amount of time on it, and you realize this is not going to work. You have to change your mind. So maybe this, with Wittgenstein, inspired me—I mean, in terms of realizing unconsciously what I so admired about him. Imagine. For years, Wittgenstein works with Bertrand Russell and G. E. Moore at Cambridge on a new philosophy. He goes to World War I, fighting for the Austrian army on the front lines. It's a terrible, demoralized army. Of course, they're defeated. Yet Wittgenstein comes away from this catastrophe with a slender manuscript called *The Tractatus*. And he thinks he's answered all the essential questions in philosophy. Thinking in his mind: "All the questions of philosophy have been answered now. We're done. We can all go home." Only to realize, years later, he was . . . wrong. A fool. Wrong about almost everything. So Wittgenstein quits philosophy and goes off to teach children. He goes into this Austrian mountain town and at first Wittgenstein is very idealistic. He thinks the children all like him. But, no, the children all hate him. [Laughter] The parents are horrible. Teaching—that doesn't work either. And so Wittgenstein comes to create another kind of philosophy. No grand truths. This is more a language philosophy looking at every particular thing that people say. Asking: Why do people say that? What does this expression really mean? Again, it's not about one incandescent overarching sort of system. It's about many different possibilities—more modern and chaotic. Well, I don't need to take you through all this, but the point here is what so amazes me about Wittgenstein as a great thinker. I mean, his bravery as a thinker, willing to do the very hardest thing. And this is to change your mind, to demolish what you have built and create something else. For me, that is what great thinking and—and art—are all about. Changing your mind. Simply changing your mind.

Parini: If I can build on what Bruce has said . . . I've always admired Wittgenstein myself. Just to imagine you had the whole world wrapped up in a ball in *The Tractatus* and then to spend two decades exploding or deconstructing your work by writing the *Philosophical Investigations*. That took courage, a kind of intellectual ferocity. I remember being first attracted to Benjamin when I was reading some letters he wrote to Gershom Scholem, his best friend who was a famous kabalistic scholar. He said, "You know, Gershom, you're always of two minds. I'm always of two dozen minds." [Laughter] What I loved about Walter Benjamin was the fact that he anticipated the fragmentation of postmodernity. That's what's most appealed to me. Pablo Neruda has a wonderful poem that begins, "My selves are many." I think this is true of all of us. I'm of about at least two dozen minds every day. I don't know which one to sit in. Or, I'm like Wallace Stevens with a mind "like a tree in which there were three blackbirds." My own tree is filled with many blackbirds. Benjamin seemed to me to anticipate this mentality. He both comes out of and resists the totalizing historical schools of Spengler or Lukacs or Erich Auerbach—the kind of positivism that gets summarized in a third-rate way by someone like A. J. Ayer in *Language, Truth, and Logic*. I find historical positivism, like philosophical positivism, somewhat old hat and false. For his part, Benjamin attracted me because he was an early thinker who was of many minds at once and who understood that there is no such thing as objective reality. There is only, as he said, the layering of subjective realities. My own work as a novelist has always involved the layering of subjective realities, trying to enter into these different subjectivities; letting each of the blackbirds in my tree to quack away for a bit. And hopefully by, as Benjamin suggested, the layering of these subjective realities, one approaches something like truth. But, you know, I love that line from Oscar Wilde's *The Importance of Being Earnest*, where he says, "The English are always degrading truths into facts." Historians and even the writers and the literary critics are so often degrading truths into facts. It's only when we start backing away from the facts and multiplying them and putting them against each other and creating not a dialogue, but an incredible cacophony of voices, that we begin to move through fragmentation toward an acceptance of the broken world that we actually occupy.

Duffy: Jay, there's one thing you said earlier. We were talking about Lukacs. And you were saying, "Well, Lukacs doesn't really speak to the postmodern world." I agree, it seems to me, Lukacs was creating this sort of battleship, this Maginot Line, of theories, all these brilliant super structures. Well, maybe that was true in his era, but I don't think it's how things operate today. It's not how people think today, and it's not true to the realities of today. Maybe I'm off course, but I think that's more or less what you were saying, Jay.

Parini: That kind of literal totalizing mentality's what got us into Iraq. I think we have to avoid that kind of thing.

Duffy: Yeah.

Lackey: Let's move to another topic. Anti-Semitism and the Holocaust are central to all of your works. Let me briefly address each one of your works individually at this point. Walter Benjamin and Gershom Scholem had a conflicted relationship. As a Jewish scholar, Scholem wanted Benjamin to embrace his Jewish heritage and to use his intellectual gifts to advance Jewish scholarship. But Benjamin understood that human identity is composed of many contradictory parts, so he could not enthusiastically embrace any single identity. What you, Jay, do so well in *Benjamin's Crossing* is to build up to that moment when Benjamin is dying and he is reflecting on his relationship with Scholem. While dying, Benjamin thinks about Scholem's theory of religious identity, which holds that Jews and Christians are essentially different. We have no way of knowing if this is what Benjamin was thinking at that time of his death. So why did your Benjamin have these thoughts on his deathbed, and how does this scene connect with the rest of the novel? Much of the novel is narrated by Scholem. Why is it significant that we get so much of the narrative from someone who was certainly close to Benjamin, but someone with whom Benjamin was in deep disagreement?

Parini: That was a way of setting a dialectic in motion. It's what I was trying to do there. Think of the trajectory of Walter Benjamin, how he begins as a kind of old school Hegelian, then he sidles his way into a kind of Marxism with some of his friends, such as Theodor Adorno. Then he gravitates, near the end, toward mystical kabalistic thought. Yet he never left any kind of thinking behind. He liked synthesizing everything. If we follow the traces of his various writings we notice that he was endlessly shape-shifting, finding different realities that wouldn't hold water and then abandoning them. Yet he kept returning to them, and then abandoning them again. On his deathbed, he was probably saying to himself: "Well, there's some truth in Marxism. There's some truth in Hegel. Maybe this dialectic is leading me somewhere." But I suspect he was moving toward a mystical understanding of reality. My sense is, looking at the letters between Gershom Scholem and Walter Benjamin, that on some level he was teasing and critiquing Scholem, suggesting to him by way of undertones: "You don't really understand what you're talking about. If you took this kabalistic mysticism seriously, you'd be living a different life." Benjamin was inherently a critic, and, like I say, he was of many minds. He allowed a play of voices—very different, even contradictory, voices—toward the end of his life. At least that's what happens in my novel. Who knows what really happened? The door is closed on history. So I'm trying—given what traces we have—to follow a path through the darkness, and see if I can arrive at some door, perhaps open it and peek in. It's my imagination peeking in.

Lackey: Nietzsche's sister married Bernhard Förster, who was a Christian anti-Semite. Elizabeth and Förster shared a dream of building a utopian community which would be free of Jews. In the late 1880s, they actually established such a community in Paraguay, and they called it Nueva Germania. Nietzsche despised Förster, and he passionately opposed his utopian community. Nietzsche did this in part because he hated anti-Semitism, as you make clear in your novel. And yet, Nietzsche's sister, who took charge of the Nietzsche Archive after Nietzsche's mental collapse, revised and even forged some of her brother's texts, thus making them acceptable—and even appealing—to Hitler and the Nazis. Your novel brilliantly builds up to the scene when Hitler visits the Nietzsche Archive and Elizabeth presents him with Nietzsche's walking stick. Why, in a novel about Nietzsche, did you shift the focus to Elizabeth, and specifically her meeting with Hitler? And why did you do all this in a novel rather than a scholarly study? Put differently, what does the novel allow you to communicate about this history-making event that you could not have communicated in a traditional biography or scholarly monograph?

Olsen: Okay. I think this is going to be my answer to why Lukacs is wrong. It's going to slant rhyme off of Jay's invocation of Wallace Stevens's poem "Thirteen Ways of Looking at a Blackbird"—that notion of needing to see reality in a multifaceted way, and also, you know, Jay's reading the poem as a postmodern. Ours is the age of polyphonic uncertainty, not the one Lukacs existed in at all, not the monologic, certain one he longed for. So, first, let me talk a little bit about the structure of *Nietzsche's Kisses*, and then quickly answer the questions you pose the best I can. *Nietzsche's Kisses* is structured in groups of three. Each chapter has a first-person section, a second-person, and a third-person. The first-person concerns the real time of Nietzsche on his deathbed, his last mad night on earth. The second-person sections are made up of Nietzsche's hallucinations, his dream states. The third-person sections are made up of Nietzsche trying to remember, to narrativize, his life. The structure of the novel, then, is insistently multivoiced—that is to say, it insistently privileges a plurality of perspectives simultaneously. The result of that structure is to bracket questions like truth, history, the world, not to mention Lukacs and his totalizing systems. [Laughter] In other words, the very structure of the novel works against any unifying view of, well, anything. It's all blackbirds all the way down. The short answer to the question of why I focused on Lisbeth and Hitler the way I did, then, is because very little is actually known about their meetings. It's historical blank space to be filled by the novelist, and the filling points to what can't be pointed to, to the moment of historiographic metafiction. You talk about the door closing on history? The door is often always-already literally closed on history. What I wanted to do was emphasize with the scene I wrote, in which Lisbeth gives Hitler Nietzsche's walking stick, Hannah Arendt's notion of the banality of evil; that you get one of the most evil guys in the history of the world behind closed doors, and he ends up talking about how nice dogs are. Who knows if that's what Lisbeth and Hitler actually talked about, of course, but if they didn't, they should have. That's the really terrifying part of Hitler: when he walked down the street, he looked just like a normal guy, except he also happened to be the leader of the Third Reich. What novels can do that scholarly studies can't? Every genre can do something that other genres can't do, or can't quite do. What's remarkable about the novel—the reason the novel exists, I think, as a genre—is that it can do three things astoundingly well that other genres can't. One is language: extended exploration of language's bliss. Poetry can do that, but for much shorter extents. Drama and film can't come close. But the more important thing is that the novel can do internal consciousness. It's a genre designed to explore internal modes of being, the circus of the mind in motion. Reading a novel, you live in another person's mind for three days, seven days, a couple weeks. What an extraordinary opportunity. What an extraordinary thing. A scholarly study can't do that, can't produce a thought-experiment about the experience of the experience of dying, the experience of a person's experience upon his deathbed if that person happens to be named Friedrich Nietzsche. The last thing novels can do that most other genres can't is bask in sense impressions. So there's that famous scene where Nietzsche protects a horse from getting whipped in Turin. We don't know anything about that day. We don't know if it was sunny, what it smelled like, what sounds were in the air. That's the novelist's job: to suggest what a moment might have felt like so a reader can imagine one version of that moment.

Lackey: Now for Bruce. Wittgenstein was Jewish. And yet he had a horribly conflicted relationship with his Jewish heritage, as you so brilliantly picture in *The World as I Found It.* This conflict manifests itself most poignantly through Wittgenstein's relationship with Max Einer, a fictional character who is a close friend of Wittgenstein's. Max, with Wittgenstein's unwitting assistance, develops some anti-Semitic views and eventually joins the S.S. Why is there this focus on anti-Semitism and the Nazis in a novel about Wittgenstein?

Duffy: One thing we do know about Wittgenstein—besides his ability to change his mind—and that's his relentless self-honesty. A quick example. One dark and stormy night, Wittgenstein called together some of his closest associates and confessed three awful things about himself. One was that he—a Jew—had been, at various times, guilty of anti-Semitism. The point is, no one could have been harder on himself. In fact, one thing that first drew me to Wittgenstein was his guilt, for example, as a guy with three brothers who committed suicide. Three. He's raised in Austria, in Vienna. He has a hugely wealthy family. And common for those times in Austria, he is a Jew whose family made the socially necessary decision to convert to Catholicism. So there was this great schism in who Wittgenstein was. I don't know all that much, to be honest, about what his personal conflicts were as far as being a Jew raised a Catholic. But I wanted to create that schism. I wanted to use this personal history as a way to explore the times, explore the dividedness, the neurosis that someone like him would have—the divided soul. As for Wittgenstein's friend Max, Max is definitely fiction. He is based on the fact that Wittgenstein was homosexual and had several muscular, working-class guys who were his friends, companions, whatever. In this way, Wittgenstein kind of reminded me of W. H. Auden, who also liked such "butch fruits," I believe they were called. Anyhow, Max is another divided soul, but more dangerous and unconscious, like Germany itself at that time. Max has come out of World War I. He was with one of the toughest fighting units that would advance offensives—men with Lugers, grenades, and flamethrowers who would lead the way. Max comes out of this, then becomes what they would call in those days "the wanderer." There was then this culture of being a hiker, a wanderer. So Max has his backpack. He's got all of his crazy, extreme religious views. And he's an anti-Semite. Here he reminded me of other people I've known who were like that . . . I had a close friend who I grew up with, really a brother when I was in high school forty years ago. Like his father, my friend hated black people—hated them. And yet, at the time, I never knew anybody better when it came to talking with black people and having a good time around them. Again, that schism. How the mind allows one kind of conduct—dreadful conduct—then somehow forgives it, creating a kind of amnesia? So in part, this was really what I was trying to do with Max—to give this very complex, I hope, portrait of a racist.

Lackey: At this point, what I want to do is segue into the question and answer section. But before I do that, what I'm going to do is get these three in a conversation with one another, and then we'll move to the Q & A. So my question for you three is this: How would you differentiate your approaches to the biographical novel from each other, and what questions do you have for each other?

Parini: I suspect we didn't quite answer a question you raised earlier, which does seem central to all of our enterprises. Why is it that all of our works often dwell on the Holocaust? *Benjamin's Crossing* is about a guy in 1940 running from the Nazis and being chased over the Pyrenees into Spain, where he is caught and commits suicide. But it's really about a man who represents, in a sense, the rational mind trying to retain a hold of rationality in an irrational world. Think of the brutality and chaos afoot: when you've got Hitler and the Nazi war machine killing millions of people in a systematic fashion—something not seen before, at least not on that scale. What I've been thinking as I've just been talking is that we, as human beings, are naturally a murderous people. Anyone who knows anything about the history of human beings knows that we club and slit each other's throats and kill each other all the time. It's what we do, one of our things, as human beings: we kill other human beings. At least a shocking number of us do, more often metaphorically than literally. What was exceptional about the Holocaust was simply the vast literal-mindedness of a regime dedicated to killing vast numbers of people: Jews, homosexuals, gypsies. Somehow systematizing that . . . Look at the number of genocides that belong to our fairly recent past. This whole country was based on the genocide of the Native Americans. Sixty million black people died in slavery. It's sad, but we're a country drenched in blood. With the Holocaust, you see this wild literalization: using the rational mind to systematize killing. And what kind of responses followed? We responded by dropping the atomic bomb on Hiroshima and Nagasaki—destroying innocent Japanese villagers. As writers, we try to come to grips with the fact that we are murderous human beings. Increasingly, since the Holocaust, we systematize this brutality. We allow our government to kill a hundred thousand Iraqis and don't even think about it much, just a few years after the fact. The terror of 9/11 gave us an excuse to commit murder on a large scale. We have assembled the largest killing machine that's ever existed—the U.S. military. There's never been an army remotely like ours, for size and destructive capability. And yet we move on, as a nation, as individuals, putting all of that to the side. We teach our classes. We study art and make pottery and make novels. But I feel like we're always living with this state of chaos, this underbelly of violence just out of view. Yet we have blood on our hands, all of us who live here and pay taxes. With the Benjamin novel, I focused on a man in flight from the murderousness of humanity systematized by the Nazis. But, you know, there's a Nazi in each of us that we're fighting. There's a state that grinds people under its wheels. We're having to contend with this all the time—or, more usually, ignore it. Fiction writing provides a way to deal with what lies beneath, out of sight: the fragmentation of our ghastly experience . . . How's that? [Laughter] Put that in your pipe and smoke it! [Laughs]

Olsen: [Laughs] I'm not going now! [Laughter]

Lackey: Maybe I should open it up for questions now. [Laughter] So do any of you have some questions for any of the panelists here?

Question 1: I'm a historian and I also try to write fiction—but not literary fiction. But I think that historians now, for the most part, are not really interested in finding out facts. I mean, we don't want to go into the unfactual, but we're more interested in, like, big patterns and how discourses construct how people think. The whole thing about the death of the author is very, very influential. And you all have been talking about "The Death of the Author" and you're kind of channeling things. But at the same time, you're talking about getting into the interiority of your characters, which I think is correct. That's what history can't do, but then what novels can do. So how do you reconcile the idea of the death of the author with your writing about the subjectivity of authors?

Olsen: This is going to take a second to answer, but I honestly think that it comes down to a grammatical misapprehension. Wittgenstein has this wonderfully instructive line that goes something like this: "One of the greatest misleading representational techniques in the language is the use of the word 'I.'" He goes on to talk about how Western thought has, by misreading grammar, created a faulty metaphysics. I'm really interested in what you're talking about: these weird authorial deployments of nouns and pronouns, and what their troubled relationship is to anything—the world, history, stable subject positions. I'm keenly aware of the problematics of the death of the author. Barthes talks about the text being a space where a number of other texts come together and clash, almost as though writers are just channeling other texts. That sounds right and not right and not-not right. I'm also interested in how, when we write a book (any kind of book) about somebody called Wittgenstein—when we write a book about somebody called Benjamin or Nietzsche—we generate a series of complications by using those nouns and pronouns. There's not really an answer in my answer, just a string of further questions and complexities. If Jay spends his time as a writer worrying about the blood we're all in up to our knees, I spend my time as a writer worrying about how nouns and pronouns misfire in interesting ways in fiction. [Laughter] And, essentially, it's the same problem. [Laughter]

Duffy: Exactly. [laughs] No doubt about it.

Lackey: Jay, do you want to respond to that?

Parini: I'm just wondering how any historians can justify their job. I mean, has somebody written the equivalent article, "The Death of the Historian"? How is it actually possible to write history in this age? I don't know how. I don't know what any historian imagines he or she is doing except creating a work of fiction. It may be based on facts, but the historians are arranging and rearranging and shuffling and building narratives and looking for patterns. When you look for patterns, it's like when you're looking at some rift in Africa. One person sees snails, the other person sees shale. Vision is ideologically grounded. So how is it possible to write history—or scientific history? You're just writing fiction without knowing it, or facing it directly.

Question 1: We spend most of our time thinking about that. [Laughter]

Parini: You make it all up.

Question 1: But also remembering the history of blood so we don't forget.

Parini: Sure.

Question 1: But also that it's all constructed.

Parini: It's the work of remembrance, which is always selective and always ideologically grounded.

Duffy: I'd say, I guess, one obvious thing, and that how we're living in an age of intense self-consciousness in which we see everything refracted in everything else. I think—if I may say so—that such a world can become crippling and overly self-referential. For example, I was talking to one of the students today in the French department who wanted to write a book, and she was going on and on and on, kind of in circles, worrying could she ever write this book. What would it be about? What would it all mean? Trying to help get her untangled, I said, "Imagine that you're in a vast library and there are all these books, every book ever written. And there's one space in that library for your book—for what you are uniquely going to create. Some small slot on the shelf." Yes, I do think that we're in a time when the book is in peril and the book industry is struggling to find another model. But I think there will always be a place for the author. The trick is to imagine that one special place—your place—in that universal library. Focus on that. Focus on the wire and not on how far you could fall.

Lackey: Did I see your hand here?

Question 2: Yeah. I'm a historian, too—a live one, not a dead one. Yet. [Laughter] I'm interested in the history of reading and the history of popular taste and the history in America in the twentieth century of popular taste for biography. I'm interested that this trend that you've identified, if you want to call it that, begins in the 1980s, and I wondered if you had any idea of why that should be. And secondly, if you saw any of your books as a part of a marketplace, in terms of an audience. I mean, did your books sell very many copies? Are they popular? And if not, is there a similar trend? Because all of your books are literary fiction. They would be classified as that, I assume, and not mass market popular fiction. Is there a similar trend or tendency towards the biographical novel in popular fiction, as well?

Duffy: [Everyone stares at Duffy.] . . . Oh. [Laughter] I don't know. You'd be better able to answer that one. Lance? Jay? Anybody.

Lackey: Well, you know, my project is very restricted because I'm focusing mainly on contemporary American biographical novels. So what's happening over in Europe is something that I'm not doing. And there have been a lot of biographical novels—Jay can talk about this—going back to the eighteenth century. The thing is that they've really started to proliferate in the last few years. Jay, is your *Last Station* a popular novel? It certainly has sold a lot. But when did it become that popular? Was it after the movie? Or was it before?

Parini: Well, it sold very well, once the movie came out. It was translated into twenty-five languages. So the bottom line was this: a lot of copies came into print!

Lackey: Is it a popular novel then?

Parini: I hope so. [Laughter] But, you know, you think back to the sixties and seventies, you had guys like Irving Stone writing *The Agony and the Ecstasy*.

Question 2: Yeah. That's a good one.

Parini: Or *Passions of the Mind* about Sigmund Freud. Those were number one bestsellers.

Question 2: *Lust for Life*, too, I guess. Vincent van Gogh.

Parini: *Lust for Life*! Vincent van Gogh! You often go back to Gore Vidal's *Lincoln*. That was a *New York Times* bestseller. It was a serious novel, and it imagines the life of Abraham Lincoln. Before that *Burr* was a huge bestseller, imagining the life of Aaron Burr. So yes, I think there's always been a kind of a public hunger for biographical fiction, at least of a certain kind. Readers like to think about other people's lives. Biography is, in many ways, one of the most ancient forms of literature. Suetonius's *Lives of the Noble Caesar* has been a bestseller for millennia, right? Or look at Vasari's *The Lives of the Artists*. The history of biography is long and deep. You'd also have to say that Suetonius was the first biographical novelist. His portrayal of Tiberius in that book has probably very little to do with the actual Tiberius, but it would make a hell of a good movie! So from that time of ancient Greece, writers have been trying to imagine lives. There were German writers working in the field of biographical fiction in the eighteenth and nineteenth centuries. It's not exactly new, but I do think that the novel after theory takes a very different turn. Even though I wasn't conscious of it, I would say that theory opened my eyes to the issue of perspective. When I started to write *The Last Station*, I thought about the fact that one could no longer adopt a positivistic, totalizing view of history. I couldn't do this, in any case. I couldn't say, "Here's what happened: Tolstoy's wife was in a bitchy mood and she started fighting with her husband. He said, 'To hell with you!' And they were throwing pots and pans at each other." That doesn't get anywhere near the complicated truth of that marriage, those lives. And it's difficult to see life steadily and whole, not now. Think of what happened in your family last weekend. Then ask the five different members of your family what happened last weekend and see what you get. This is where history comes in. This is real history. This is reality processed by memory. It becomes fiction.

Lackey: Anne?

Question 3: My question is kind of based off of two things. Last night, Jay, you mentioned that you did change a lot, but you didn't dare mess with Tolstoy's actual words. Today, you said that in some ways, we have a duty to change the past. I'm kind of struggling with those two concepts together. In what ways can we change the past and with which people? That also ties into my problems with how honesty and dishonesty function in this discourse of truth in fiction.

Parini: Last night I was talking in Morris [University of Minnesota, Morris] to some students. I mentioned the fact that when I wrote *The Last Station*, I felt shy about putting words in Tolstoy's mouth. I decided not to have Tolstoy be one of the characters speaking in the narrative per se, and I didn't want to write as Tolstoy. It wasn't possible. So whenever I had Tolstoy speak, I actually used quotations from Tolstoy. You might consider my novel the red letter edition of Tolstoy. I did, of course, make up conversations where he talked. Nevertheless, I put those conversations in created contexts, as some other character recollecting the dialogue. So that was a kind of idiosyncratic factor of *The Last Station*, that I decided to stick with the actual words of Tolstoy always. Because he happened to have a lot of people reporting what he said, I knew the sorts of things he probably said in reaction to situations. Sometimes I just took things from Tolstoy's fiction, as when I wanted to know what Tolstoy thought about death; I simply stripped out a page at the end of *The Death of Ivan Ilyich* and plugged it into my narrative. But you raise a very interesting thing here about truth or lies. I would say I'm more interested in whether something is authentic or inauthentic than true or false. I'm trying to create in my novels an experience for the reader that feels authentic. It's not "real." It's a made-up book, a novel. It's playing with reality. It's trying to imagine history, but in calling itself a novel, it gives you the license to create. By the time I turned to Benjamin and Melville, I felt at greater liberty to invent voices. I said to myself, "To hell with reporting actual conversations. I'm going to make it all up." [Laughter] So I made up their conversations based on what I thought they might have said. Even with the personal history of Melville, for instance, I asked myself: Does this seem to you like something that could have happened to Herman Melville? We know, for example, that Herman Melville briefly jumped ship in the South Seas on the island of Nuku Hiva and that he was kidnapped by a tribe of bisexual cannibals and that after several weeks he escaped. He writes about this in "fiction," which he calls a memoir, in *Typee*. He makes up names, but he says, "This is my own true experience." But he's making it up! When I was writing my novel, I thought, "What more fun could there be than imagining being kidnapped by a tribe of bisexual cannibals?" [Laughter] Melville goes there, in a sense, but doesn't go far enough. I took it further and played with it. There's an intentional playfulness there. The only truth I'm worried about is: does it seem authentic to the reader, as something that might have happened? What would it be like if you were kidnapped by a tribe of bisexual cannibals? What would you do? Go with it?

Duffy: Alas, I cannot speak to bisexual cannibals. In my case, I was being cavalier earlier when I said, "Do you really care how many sisters and brothers Wittgenstein had?" In other words, the fact is that I drastically reduced that number. On the other hand, I was obsessive with the tremendous amount of period detail required. I wanted the sort of details where the reader would think, "Wow. Where'd he ever find that?" The thing that was absolutely nonnegotiable was having the book be true to Wittgenstein's thought and to the trajectory of his thoughts. Here I wanted the reader not just to understand these ideas as "thoughts," but to feel them as real human problems. How did Wittgenstein come up with these ideas? Why did this idea occur to him? How did the realities of his life produce such unique thinking? Here I wanted the reader to experience, I hoped, the existential sense of being Wittgenstein, feeling that pain, that heat. In other words, realizing that ideas really do respond to life realities. Anxieties and many, many other things. So I guess I'm saying, in a long-winded way, that it's not all bullshit. [Laughs]

Olsen: I'm saying I don't know where literature ends and the bullshit begins. I would therefore answer in a faintly different way. A very strange thing happened in intellectual history after World War II. Think of Hemingway as the archetypal modernist macho guy who needed to write 500 words before he went out to fish. Then think about what happens after, say, the forties and fifties. There are suddenly whole generations of writers that want to write and do so, not by following Hemingway's path, but by going to college, perhaps even graduate school, and thereby become immersed in philosophy, aesthetics, and literary theory. That totally screws you up, because once you've read that stuff, you're infected. It's like biting the apple and being forced from the Garden of Eden. The flaming swords come down behind you, and you may want to get back in, but tough luck. Such knowledge gets you to think about certain problems in ways that, let's say, Hemingway would never have contemplated them. So I feel super uncomfortable talking about such ideas as "authentic" and "inauthentic," or "honesty" and "dishonesty," or "truth" and "untruth," because I honestly don't know what those words mean, can't point to their signifieds, can't think past a web of poststructuralist complications, nuancings, demythifications. I know what such words are supposed to mean, of course. But I'm not sure what they actually do. And I keep translating them from the realm of metaphysics into questions of narrativity—who's structuring the story, from what perspective, out of what ideology, for what reasons. That gives you a different set of questions to ask as you're moving into a novel. It isn't, of course, that I didn't do a lot of research on *Nietzsche's Kisses*. I read all the biographies I could get my hands on, read Nietzsche lots of times, traveled through Germany and Switzerland and Italy taking copious notes about the places that he spent parts of his life. But when I sat down to translate all of that into a novel—and this goes back to what I started off by saying—what I kept being metacognitive about was that what I was really doing wasn't getting at any "authenticity," any "truth," about Nietzsche. I was getting at what my sense of Nietzsche was at a certain time. And so we're back to those nouns and pronouns. For me, writing fiction amounts to exploring what we don't know. So I'm much more confused than Jay.

Lackey: Ande?

Question 4: I have been noticing some interesting parallels among how you each approached your subjects that you're writing about. In traditions of European thought, typically history and philosophy have looked at what is essential and what is unified about how we look at events, like identity having its central qualities. You've all looked at thinkers whose systems of thought have tried to de-essentialize reality and look at identity as being dynamic and fractious and not unified. Part of that has been each of them examining language as a symbolic system that is culturally embedded. I think that because each of you have looked at racism as well that there has been this sort of interesting thought that has been percolating as you were talking. As authors, you're in a unique position to use language to expose conflicts about how we interpret cultural meaning and show where we are in conflict, like looking at racism. There are ideas we have about people that to us are correct because we know things about ourselves and our culture, but are incorrect to those people. As authors, you've examined the nature of meaning, in a way. I'm wondering how, when you've approached your novels, if you've seen ways in which historical novels are in a unique position to help readers cultivate a multicultural consciousness. That was a gigantic question, for which I apologize. [Laughs] The last part is the part that I was really trying to frame properly.

Duffy: That's good, because you will probably not like the answer to this. I think, at least in the way I write, that I'm consumed with what's going on with the characters. In other words, without any cultural agenda. It's hard to write within the confines of any agenda. In fact, this is what I was objecting to in Lukacs. Anyhow, I don't operate in this way, and to be perfectly honest, I can't imagine that many writers do. But maybe you'll say that I'm wrong. [Laughs]

Olsen: I don't say that anybody's wrong. That was the most awesome question, by the way.

Duffy: That was a good question.

Olsen: I'm not sure that I was really thinking about this when I was writing the Nietzsche book, not sure that I really wasn't, but I am sure that the Nietzsche book was thinking about these things. So here's the short version of Nietzsche's narrative of Western philosophy: everything was just fine before Plato, then everything went to hell in a hand basket. The reason for this was Plato tried to essentialize, tried to categorize and stabilize. The thing Nietzsche found so alluring about the pre-Socratics like Heraclitus was their sense that essentializing simply didn't exist. [Alarm goes off] The constitution of reality, of lived experience for somebody like Heraclitus . . . Excuse me. My alarm's going off. I'll be right with you. Apparently I'm about to make a very important point about Western culture. [Laughter] The constitution of reality, of lived experience for somebody like Heraclitus is change. Transformation is the only thing that is consistent in the world. One of the things that I find really alluring about thinkers like Wittgenstein and Nietzsche is precisely their move to de-essentialize, to trouble assumptions, to challenge, to take nothing for granted. The result is always going to be of multiplicity. I would imagine race, then, to be a tremendously troublesome concept for Nietzsche, because race is a cultural attempt to essentialize in the face of a profuse, continuous changing pluriverse.

Lackey: Rachel, go ahead.

Question 5: You've all briefly mentioned your research process, either today or, in Jay Parini's case, last night at Morris. Then after mentioning your research process, you've all made comments about how "that wasn't what ultimately determined how you pictured the man you were writing about." So I'm wondering how important your research was to you, and what parts of it were the most important. What did really have an impact on your book?

Duffy: Was that to me?

Question 5: Any of you!

Duffy: Well, when I started *The World as I Found It*, it was before the Internet, so you didn't have all this ready digital access to the library. Luckily, I was living outside of Washington D.C., near the Library of Congress. So there my wife and I would go on Friday nights, off to the Library of Congress for a late-night Xeroxing party. Some date. I'd get $50.00 in dimes [Laughter] and we would go in there and start madly checking out books. Then we'd start photocopying them until I ran out of dimes. [Laughter] So I read all kinds of things. I also looked at a lot of period photos. I would just pore over photos, which just give you a tremendous amount of knowledge if you really look at them, for example, to imagine how the heat felt on the walls of Cambridge, what those bricks felt like. I read a number of period diaries and journals to really get a sense of what people were saying, how they really spoke, syntax and the like. Meanwhile, at the county library, I was checking out bags of books. Imagine that, having to stand behind this lunatic checking out seventy-five books. That's basically what I did with *The World as I Found It*.

Parini: I suspect that many of us really enjoy the idea of historical research. Although I make jokes about facts, I enjoy them, and I try in my biographical novels to stick with the agreed upon facts. So if I say that Herman Melville boarded a ship called *The Something* on this date, he will have done that. Melville took a train in the spring of 1857 from Rome to Florence. I went to the trouble of finding out what were the train schedules and how much did it cost for a ticket. I like to line up all the facts. You've got to get your marbles in your bag to write a novel. But then you arrange them; play with them. What did these things mean—facts on their own, the agreed upon facts? The date when Tolstoy left home matters, but what did it mean? And that's what you're trying to get at. You have to imagine those facts. You have to think of what they actually mean. That's what the writing in fiction is about. Fiction simply is about ordering the facts and imagining them: the motives, how things went down, and why they went down. As novelists, we're doing the same thing that historians are doing. They're just working slightly differently, with different genre restrictions and conventions. But I think we all build from research. Research is essential, and a huge amount of research is the baseline from which we begin to work.

Olsen: None of us could have written what we wrote without extensive sorts of research. Boots-on-the-ground research opens up an extraordinary number of doors. It's beyond richness to stand in the cramped room Nietzsche died in, for instance, and look at the bed, how the light fell. Fiction's all about what if. So I don't think any of us would deny how important the facts are, but the kinds of facts for me that are exciting are the ones that stimulate exactly those questions, rather than pin down any answers.

Duffy: One thing that I might add, talking about all of these facts. As I said, I'd check out all of these books, then pore over them, basically gorging myself. Then, almost closing my eyes, I'd write without looking at any of them. Why? Because you can be so seduced by the facts, so intimidated by the facts that you don't really reimagine the world as you must.

Lackey: It looks like our time is up, so let us end there. Thank you Jay, Bruce, and Lance for sharing your thoughts with us. And thank you, Ann, for having us.

Self-Interview: JP talks to Jay Parini

Jay Parini / 2013

From a self-interview on January 3, 2013. Reprinted by permission.

Sitting in my study in Vermont, on a snowy day, I looked over my desk at the Green Mountains and thought about the fact that interviews never really ask you what you want to be asked, or not always. A figure called J.P. arrived on the scene, sat on my leather couch, and put some questions to me. They seemed exactly what I wanted to answer at that moment, and the results are below.

JP: How old are you?
Parini: Almost sixty-five. In other words, old enough to know better.

JP: Know what?
Parini: I should know by now how to solve many problems, answer many questions more appropriately, understand my writing and learning process more consciously. I always seem, to myself, a beginner. Only last night I returned from Scotland. I visited my old haunts, in St. Andrews, walked around the old town, the university where I spent seven years. I had dinner with my old tutor, Anthony Ashe. I felt like I was just beginning to understand a few things.

JP: Ashe is retired now?
Parini: Yes, but I realize how much I owe to him and others I met when I was young. When I met him, I was twenty. His seminars in English poetry shifted my whole sense of myself. He brought a quality of intelligence to bear on a text that inspired me. I decided to refigure my life. Instead of going to law school or into business, I made a thoroughgoing commitment to literary studies, to writing poetry, to reading books with care. I returned to St. Andrews in 1970 with a sense of urgency. I wanted to make myself into

149

a writer. This involved reading a good deal, talking over poems and novels, criticism, with people who understood this stuff. I was very lucky, too. It was a good place and time. I met an astonishing range of writers, including Borges and Neruda. I found a writing mentor in Alastair Reid, who introduced me to both of these Latin American writers. I had some initial luck, publishing reviews and poems in Scottish journals. I still remember the immense thrill when I got an acceptance from *Scottish International*, a journal in Edinburgh. I nearly ran around the town at top speed. My first little book of poems came out with a Scottish press.

JP: You wrote fiction, too?
Parini: A terrible comic novel in the vein of Evelyn Waugh, seven hundred awful pages. It was never published. I wrote another novel about Vietnam that was never published, thank God. My first novel, *The Love Run*, was—unfortunately—published.

JP: Why unfortunately?
Parini: Because I didn't know enough about fiction, and the novel was thin, silly, and embarrassing. It made a little money, however, and that came in handy when my wife and I needed a house. We had a down payment.

JP: Has writing in so many genres been a bad thing?
Parini: Only for my reputation. This is a specialized society. Ever since the Industrial Revolution, there has been a mania for doing one thing, over and over. You're the man who punches holes. You write poems. You over there, you're the novelist. And so forth. I prefer the old European model of the writer—someone like Schiller or Goethe, not that I'm in their league. But they wrote plays, poems, novels, criticism, philosophy. It was commonplace for writers to express different ideas in a multitude of genres. Even in English, one thinks of Lawrence, Hardy, Graves, and so many others. I've tried to keep poetry—writing and reading it—the center of my intellectual focus. I mainly teach poetry. But some ideas or emotions demand other forms. One is able to express oneself in poems, in fiction, in essays, in plays, in different ways. Each genre brings out fresh colors in a writer. I only wish I'd spent more time on plays. I've written two of them; but they're apprentice work. I'm only just learning to write screenplays with a degree of sophistication. I'd better, in old age, focus on poems and novels. I'll probably write essays as well. I love essays.

JP: So what's next?
Parini: I just finished a short biography of Jesus.

JP: Really?
Parini: It sounds absurd, given my previous work. But in fact I've been a practicing Anglican for many decades, beginning in St. Andrews. I studied the Greek New Testament as a graduate student, and have read widely in modern theology: Rudolf Bultmann, Paul Tillich, Karl Barth, and Martin Buber. I've continued to read theological books over the years. I've also read Buddhist scriptures and thinkers, and these have been influential. I'm a fan of the *Tao Te Ching*. In short, my religious and philosophical views marry pretty closely with Eliot's in *Four Quartets*. Those poems brought into play a range of theological and philosophical concerns. I regard time as an illusion, and I hope to rest in God.

JP: What do you mean by God?
Parini: Echoing Tillich, I would say that God is our ultimate concern, the ground of our being. That sounds rather painfully abstract, and it must remain so. I'm not being evasive, but I do think that the separation between the living and the dead is paper thin, and that the word God is useful in describing a reality deeper than the one we inhabit consciously. Christianity offers a way of being in the world that comprehends and encourages daily transformations. It's about imitating Christ. This means allowing for that change of heart represented by the Greek word *metanoia*. It's not unlike Buddhist enlightenment: one gets beyond the petty self, and reaches for something larger, entering a larger consciousness. What especially appeals to me about Christianity is the idea of the gradually realizing kingdom of God. It grows on us day by day. It deepens.

JP: So how does one accomplish these things?
Parini: Eliot suggests "prayer, observance, discipline, thought and action."

JP: How do you regard fundamentalist Christians?
Parini: My father was one, so I regard them with sympathy. But I dislike all forms of literalism. Atheism and fundamentalism are two sides of the same literalist coin. I'm in search of *mythos*, which is the Greek word for story. The story of Jesus is a good one. He shows us a way to deal with suffering, and life is suffering. That's a key Buddhist idea, and there is no way around

it. We must take that on fully. But we can move through suffering. Robert Frost once said: "The only way out is through." I believe that. Yet I'm also a fairly Emersonian fellow: I believe in transcendence. "The highest revelation is that God is in every man," Emerson said. There is a divine spark in every person. Letting that spark grow into a flame, a holy bonfire, is the work of the soul.

JP: But you consider yourself a political activist, don't you?

Parini: I wouldn't go that far; but I've been involved in antiwar activities since the time of Vietnam. I admire Noam Chomsky a great deal, especially in his understanding of the responsibility of intellectuals. He once suggested that people who are capable of working with ideas, with using words, have the duty to analyze society in honest ways, to expose the lies of governments, to look for motives and hidden intentions. I don't want to live my life in a paranoid fashion, nor am I unpatriotic. I believe in the key democratic ideas of the American Founding Fathers. Over many years I saw my friend Gore Vidal—a writer I admire—thinking in a certain paranoid way at times. Paranoia is unhealthy. I want to try my best to speak out, when I can, for justice, for peace, for human equality. I care deeply about the environment, and I've written about this a lot, especially in poems and essays. I have tried, in my reviewing and essay-writing, to support what I would consider enlightenment values. But these are also Christian values. The Sermon on the Mount is a loud call to justice. It asks us to behave in radical ways: turning the other cheek, giving a man our coat if he asks for our shirt. The Beatitudes are built on the idea of karma: mercy comes to those who are merciful. The poor in spirit as well as those without cash will inherit the earth. This is challenging stuff.

JP: What writers inspire you?

Parini: I don't have enough time to mention them. But I've learned a great deal from Wendell Berry. His essays seem to me a remarkable product of the American mind going at full tilt. He writes in the tradition of Thoreau. I'm amazed by his eloquence. I spend a lot of time reading poetry, of course. I never tire of the Book of Psalms, Donne and Herbert, Hopkins, Whitman, Frost, Eliot, Stevens. I read Adrienne Rich often. I love the work of Heaney, Ted Hughes, Charles Wright, Charles Simic, Louise Glück, and so many others.

JP: What novelists do you read?

Parini: Waugh, Iris Murdoch, Roth and Bellow, Malamud, Singer, Morrison. I often go back to Thomas Mann and Tolstoy. I've loved various Italian and Latin American writers, such as Calvino and Marquez. I read a lot of contemporary British writers, including Julian Barnes and Ian McEwan. I also read my friends closely: Ann Beattie, Julia Alvarez, Erica Jong, Robert Cohen, John Irving, Chris Bohjalian. I have many friends who write, and I like seeing what they do. Literature is conversation. I feel close to any number of poets, many of whom are friends, such as Michael Collier, Greg Delanty, and Richard Kenney. I depend on these friendships in so many ways. I miss Gore Vidal, who died last summer.

JP: How did you meet Vidal?
Parini: I was living in Italy, three decades ago. I moved into a village next to Amalfi, into a small villa overlooking the sea. My wife and I had two little children, one of them a newborn. I remember looking up from our terrace at the massive palace on the cliff, a five-story white structure that clung to the rocks rather perilously, or so it seemed. I asked our local tobacconist in Amalfi who lived there. Some duke? He said, "No, Vidal. Gore Vidal, *lo scritore.*" I asked if he ever mixed with the hoi polloi, the locals, and he told me Vidal walked past my house every day and came into town to buy a newspaper. He then proceeded to the bar next door for a drink, where he read the paper before going home. I left a note for him, explaining I was an American writer who had moved to the coast. I'd be there for at least six months. If there was any chance to meet him, that would be a pleasure. That very evening he pounded on our door. "Come for dinner," he said, when I opened it. I was somewhat startled. We went up to the house for dinner, and Vidal stopped by nearly every day in the afternoon, taking me into town for a drink. Often we kept talking till the wee hours. A friendship developed. I don't think he had a lot of company in that big house, except for Howard, his companion of many decades. In the ensuing years, we talked every week on the phone, sometimes every day. We visited each other, traveled here and there: Austria, London, Oxford, New York, Key West. I often spent time at his villa in Ravello. He came to see me in Vermont. It was a long and rewarding friendship, for me. I hope for him, too. I learned a great deal from our conversations, from reading his novels and essays.

JP: What about Robert Penn Warren?
Parini: I met him soon after coming to Dartmouth in 1975. He was a friend of Richard Eberhart, the poet, who brought us together. We liked each other,

and I began to visit him frequently. I'd spend a night or two at his summer home in West Wardsboro, Vermont, where he is buried. In later years, my family and I often spent a few days at the New Year with the Warrens, Red and Eleanor, and with their children, Gabe and Rosanna. I treasure memories of long walks in the woods with Red. We'd talk about books and writing. He was the chief model in my life: university teacher, poet, novelist, critic. His generosity with young people was stunning. He was among the gentlest, the kindest people I ever met. I had so many good times with him, sitting at his table in Vermont or Connecticut. We were friends, and that meant a lot to me. I love his poetry, especially in the later phase, when he wrote such vivid, autobiographical, and quirky philosophical verse. He had read everything, and that impressed me. We shared a love of Hardy, Auden, Eliot, and Frost. He introduced me to the work of such writers as Allen Tate and John Crowe Ransom, whom I came to admire deeply. I have such lovely recollections of long dinners at his house with people like Cleanth Brooks and Saul Bellow. Warren's generation was a remarkable one. These were profoundly interesting and interested writers, with a moral edge.

JP: What do your workdays look like?

Parini: I'm a believer in habit. I depend on my grooves, which lead me through the years. After an early breakfast of toast (with almond butter) and tea, I go to a café in Middlebury, where I have a cup of coffee and talk to people and write, usually at the same table overlooking the Otter Creek, a river that runs through the center of town. My colleague and friend Rob Cohen is always there, and we chew the fat, discuss projects, trade stories, grumble about the state of the world. I try to get a few pages written every day. I have poems, which I write by hand, in progress in my notebook. I do prose on the laptop. At lunchtime I go to the gym, where I work out. Three days a week I play basketball, as I've done for nearly forty years. In the afternoon, I sit in my office at the college. I teach classes or meet with students or write. I often do some shopping and cook dinner. After dinner, I read or watch films. Once a week or so I have dinner with Julia Alvarez and her husband, Bill Eichner, who live almost next door. We're very close friends. Julia is a major part of my life. I work most days. Only on Sundays do I rarely do much of anything, apart from attending services at St. Stephens, a local Episcopal church. I like to walk on Sunday afternoons.

JP: You exercise a lot.

Parini: If you can't make time for exercise, you have to make time for illness.

JP: What about future works?

Parini: I have recently finished a ghost story called *Galliano's Ghost*—a novel set on Lake Champlain. The biography of Jesus that I wrote will appear in the summer. I am working on a life of Gore Vidal and a novel about Franklin Roosevelt. I also have a new book of poems, which I plan to called *Ordinary Time*, a liturgical phrase. There's no rush on any of these, but don't tell that to my publishers.

JP: How do you hope to be remembered?

Parini: As a writer and teacher who did the best he could with limited gifts. We proceed, as Frost once said, on insufficient knowledge. I'm the best example I know of that principle in action.

Index

Printed in the United States
By Bookmasters